D-DAY

IN NUMBERS

D-DAY
IN NUMBERS

JACOB F. FIELD

MICHAEL O'MARA BOOKS LIMITED

First published in Great Britain in 2014 by
Michael O'Mara Books Limited
9 Lion Yard
Tremadoc Road
London SW4 7NQ

A CIP catalogue record for this book is available from the British Library.

Papers used by Michael O'Mara Books Limited are natural, recyclable
products made from wood grown in sustainable forests. The manufacturing
processes conform to the environmental regulations of the country of origin.

ISBN: 978-1-78243-205-0 in hardback print format
ISBN: 978-1-78243-239-5 in ebook format

1 2 3 4 5 6 7 8 9 10

Designed and typeset by Design 23
Illustrations by David Woodroffe

Printed and bound by CPI Group (UK) Ltd, Croydon, CR0 4YY

www.mombooks.com

To Emily

Contents

Contents

Introduction

ON 6 JUNE 1944, THE MOST COMPLEX and ambitious invasion in military history took place. The D-Day Landings were the culmination of years of planning and preparation. The invading Allies would disembark at five landing zones code-named Utah, Omaha, Gold, Juno, and Sword. In addition airborne troops would be landed behind enemy lines. They would combine to attempt to drive the Germans out of Normandy. If this effort succeeded then they would pave the way for the liberation of the rest of France and the Low Countries, and eventually a strike into Germany. Failure would delay the end of the war and strain the alliance with the Soviet Union, eager for the western Allies to open up another front against Germany. The invading Allies were facing an enemy that had had years to build up their defences, turning cities into fortresses and scattering the beaches with thousands of obstacles.

Success at Normandy demanded the bravery, skill, and cunning of hundreds of thousands of Allied soldiers, sailors, and airmen. The majority of the servicemen were drawn from the United Kingdom, the United States, and Canada, but many other nationalities played a role. From French Resistance fighters, to Polish tank crews, to Jewish commandos who had fled from persecution in German territory, the Battle for Normandy was a multi-national victory. It was a massive strategic effort, requiring the careful integration of land, maritime, and aerial units. The Allies also had to consider the huge logistical problem of unloading tens of thousands of men, as well as the supplies, equipment, and vehicles they needed to fight. D-Day was also at the centre of one of the great triumphs of the British intelligence service, whose campaign of misinformation was crucial in hiding Allied invasion plans from the Germans.

D-Day in Numbers tells the story of the invasion of Normandy through the statistics and figures associated with the campaign. It begins with the origins of World War II and continues past D-Day to detail the victorious drive through France and into Germany. The numbers are staggering: from the 156,000 Allied troops landed in France on 6 June to the seventeen million cubic metres of concrete the Germans used to construct the network of fortifications protecting the Atlantic coast. Others show the human sacrifice of the conflict; the 10,000 Allied casualties on D-Day, or the 19,890 civilian deaths in the Battle for Normandy. This book details the equipment that helped the Allies win victory, from the ingenious 'swimming tanks' to the

'Mulberry' temporary harbours. Individual units are examined, from the fearsome British Commandos to the notorious Twelfth SS Panzer Division *Hitlerjugend*. The roles of key figures are examined, like Brigadier General Theodore Roosevelt III, the oldest man ashore on D-Day, Bill Millin, who landed in Normandy playing the bagpipes, and Joan Pujol Garcia, the Catalan double agent who helped the Allies to deceive Germany. *D-Day in Numbers* reveals the sheer scale of the preparation, execution, and impact of the event that shaped the outcome of World War II.

Chapter 1:
The War in Europe So Far

£6,600,000,000

THE 11 NOVEMBER 1918 armistice ended the fighting in World War I. It took several months for the Allied Powers (led by France, the United States, and the United Kingdom) and Germany to negotiate the Treaty of Versailles, signed on 28 June 1919. Its major point was Article 231, the 'War Guilt' clause, under which Germany accepted responsibility for starting the war. She was liable to pay reparations for the damages the Allies suffered, valued in 1921 at £6,600,000,000, to be paid in a mixture of cash and commodities such as coal. Allied troops were to occupy the Rhineland for fifteen years. This region was in western Germany and an important centre of industry. Germany was to cede territory in Europe, give up its colonies, and was forbidden from joining with Austria. Versailles stripped Germany of its military capacity by limiting its army to 100,000 and its navy to 15,000. Her armed forces were forbidden to use armed aircraft, tanks, or submarines. Many Germans found the treaty offensive, believing that Germany, never fully defeated in the field, had been 'stabbed in the back' by politicians. During the Great Depression of the 1930s high unemployment and hyperinflation struck Germany, leading to a rise in support for radical groups like Adolf Hitler's Nazis. One of Hitler's promises was to tear up Versailles, and restore Germany's greatness. As for the reparations, they were suspended in 1932 due to the Depression, and never resumed. Germany only paid one-eighth of their value. Once in power Hitler sought to reverse Versailles; he built up the size and strength of the German armed forces, in 1936 he remilitarized the Rhineland, and in 1938 Germany annexed Austria.

10,000,000 copies

ADOLF HITLER'S *MEIN KAMPF* ('My Struggle') was a mixture of autobiography, ideology, and political manifesto, steeped in a virulent mixture of anti-Semitism and anti-Communism. Hitler started the work while he was imprisoned after a failed uprising in 1923. It was published in 1925, and sold 23,000 copies in five years. As Hitler rose to power, the book's popularity and circulation increased.

By 1945 around ten million copies had been sold or distributed. Royalties from *Mein Kampf* meant Hitler built up a large private fortune.

288 seats

ON 5 MARCH 1933, the last free elections before the Nazi takeover of Germany were held. Hitler had been chancellor since January, but his National Socialist Workers' Party did not have a majority. Despite this, Hitler had been able to repress the Communist Party by arresting its members and launching a propaganda campaign against them. On Election Day Nazi supporters roamed the streets, attempting to sway the vote with the threat of violence. Despite this, the Nazis won only 288 seats with forty-four per cent of the vote. This left them thirty-six seats short of a majority in the *Reichstag*, meaning they had to form a coalition. This did not stop Hitler from passing the Enabling Act on 23 March, which allowed his cabinet to pass laws without consulting the *Reichstag*. Trade unions were banned and other political parties were suppressed or forced to disband. On 2 August 1934, the head of state, President Paul von Hindenburg, died. His office was abolished and merged with that of the chancellor. Hitler now became *Führer und Reichskanzler* – head of government and head of state. Hitler became Supreme Commander of the German armed forces, who would be made to swear an oath of loyalty to Hitler. In 1935 the Nazi symbol, the swastika, was proclaimed to be Germany's sole national flag. In just a few years Germany had transformed from a multi-party democracy into a militaristic, single-party fascist dictatorship.

10 years old

THE HITLER YOUTH was founded in 1922 as the youth wing of the Nazis. After 1936 all German boys over the age of ten were expected to join its junior section, the *Deutsches Jungvolk* ('German Youth'). There was a similar organization for girls and young women called the *Bund Deutscher Mädel* ('League of German Maidens'). By 1939 membership of the Hitler Youth was made compulsory for all boys between ten and eighteen. It placed great emphasis on preparing boys for military service, as well as inculcating them with Nazi ideology. After the Hitler Youth many boys would go on to join the elite Nazi group, the *Schutzstaffel* (SS). As World War II went on and German manpower was depleted, the Hitler Youth became a military reserve force. Many of its teenage members fought in the Battle of Normandy and young boys were involved in the doomed defence of Berlin.

158,962,555,217,826,360,000 settings

The German Enigma machine, which was used to encode messages, had nearly 159 quintillion possible settings. The machine was developed for commercial use in the 1920s by the German engineer Arthur Scherbius. Its military application quickly became apparent. The Enigma relied on a series of rotating wheels, which scrambled letters entered into the machine's keyboard by the operator. The resulting scrambled message, an intelligible mess of letters, was then communicated via Morse Code. It could only be decoded if the recipient knew the exact settings used when it was written. Once the fighting began, the German armed forces usually changed their Enigma settings daily, believing it would make their communications impossible to decode. Events later in the war would show this confidence was misplaced.

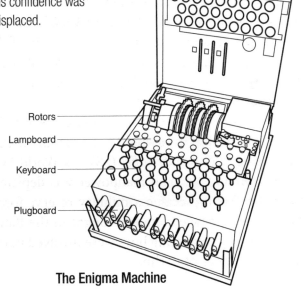

Rotors

Lampboard

Keyboard

Plugboard

The Enigma Machine

3,500,000 shelters

SIR JOHN ANDERSON was the government official responsible for preparing Britain for bombing raids before the outbreak of World War II. His name was given to the Anderson shelter, designed by a team at the Institution of Civil Engineers. It was the main air-raid shelter used by the British public. From February 1939 until the end of the war, over 3.5 million shelters were erected. They were made of fourteen sheets of corrugated iron, which formed a shelter buried four feet into the ground. These shelters could hold up to six people. They were given free to households earning less than £250 per year. The Morrison shelter was designed to be used indoors. It was a heavy table fortified by a steel plate and wire-mesh sides. This shelter was issued as a kit assembled at home. By the end of the war around 600,000 had been distributed.

£1 8s per week

THE WOMEN'S LAND ARMY (WLA) was created during World War I to organize female replacements for male agricultural workers who were fighting. With conflict looming again, the WLA was revived in June 1939. They were paid a weekly wage of one pound and eight shillings and also received room and board. Through a mixture of volunteers and conscription, the WLA grew to 80,000 members. Most were from rural areas but around one-third came from large cities. Female labour was vital to the British economy during the war. Between 1939 and 1943 four out of five people added to the labour force were women who had not previously worked full-time.

387 feet

GLIWICE (OR GLEIWITZ) RADIO TOWER is the tallest wooden structure in Europe, standing nearly four hundred feet tall. Built in 1935, it resembles the Eiffel Tower – except with a wooden framework. Although now in Poland, in 1939 the tower was in Germany. It was the focus of Operation Himmler, a series of events the Germans staged to give the impression of Polish aggression and give Hitler a public justification for invading Poland. On 31 August, a group of Germans, dressed in Polish uniforms, staged a fake raid on the tower and broadcast a brief anti-German message. Several prisoners from Dachau concentration camp were poisoned, dressed in Polish uniforms, and riddled with bullets to give the impression there had been a firefight. That day there were several other faked attacks on other locations on the border. On 1 September, Hitler addressed the *Reichstag*, and used these incidents as a pretence for launching an invasion he had long been planning. France and the United Kingdom had vowed to declare war on Germany if they invaded Poland, but Hitler did not believe they would act on this threat.

11 cavalry brigades

POLAND HAD LONG EXPECTED a German invasion. She had built up her military capacity to nearly one million men. Cavalry units still formed ten per cent of their strength. They were mainly used as mobile infantry and for reconnaissance (it is a misconception that they charged German tanks with sabres and lances). The German invasion on 1 September 1939 caught the Polish by surprise and they were unable to mobilize all of their forces. At eight in the morning German troops had crossed into Poland. They were the first of an invading army of 1.5 million. The Germans had nearly six times as many aircraft and over three times as many tanks, and generally enjoyed technical superiority. On 3 September, the United Kingdom and France declared war on Germany. They could do little to help Poland, whose armies fought valiantly but were pushed steadily back. On 17 September, a Soviet army of 800,000 invaded from the east. This was no surprise to Germany. Germany and the Soviet Union had signed a secret pact in August 1939 carving up Eastern Europe into separate spheres of influence. Fighting ended on 6 October. Over ninety-five per cent of the Polish armed forces were lost – dead, wounded, or captured. Two hundred thousand Polish civilians were killed. Poland was wiped from the map and divided between Germany, Slovakia, and the Soviet Union.

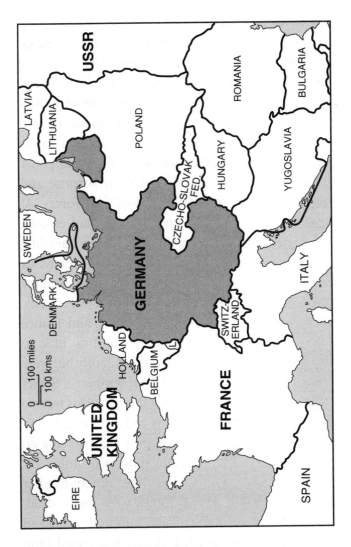

European Borders Before World War II

44 formal declarations of war

GERMANY INVADED POLAND without declaring war. Two days later the United Kingdom and France declared war on Germany as a result. Following this, there were forty-three other formal declarations of war made during World War II. Some of the lesser-known declarations include Albania declaring war on the United States on 17 December 1941, Bolivia's declaration of war against the Axis powers (Germany, Italy and Japan) on 2 April 1943, and San Marino formally entering the conflict against Germany on 21 September 1944. The final declaration of World War II was made on 8 August 1945, when the Soviet Union declared war on Japan.

103,000 teachers evacuated

OPERATION PIED PIPER was a British effort to move children, mothers, pregnant women, and the disabled from cities at risk of being bombed to safer areas. In addition, 103,000 teachers were evacuated. In total, 3.5 million people were relocated. The evacuations began on 1 September, two days before the declaration of war on Germany. Many children stayed in cities; for example, 800,000 children remained in London.

1,500 observation posts

THE ROYAL OBSERVER CORPS was a volunteer civilian organization that manned over 1,500 observation posts in Britain, day and night, for nearly the whole duration of the war. At its peak 33,100 male and 1,000 female volunteers were on the look-out for enemy aircraft.

51 ships sunk

DURING THE BATTLE OF THE ATLANTIC, Axis and Allied powers vied for maritime supremacy as they both sought to prevent supplies reaching land. German submarines (U-boats) were highly effective at locating and sinking enemy ships, hunting in 'wolf packs', which descended on Allied convoys with brutal swiftness. The most lethal was *U-48*, launched six months before the conflict began. In the course of twelve patrols, from 1939 to 1941, *U-48* sank fifty-five ships with a combined tonnage of 321,000. As the war went on, the Allies adopted new tactics and weapons that limited the effectiveness of the U-boats, meaning more shipments got through to Britain unharmed. In total, U-boats sank 2,603 merchant ships (with the loss of 30,000 lives and a combined tonnage of 13.5 million) and 175 naval vessels.

28,000 crew killed

OUT OF 40,900 MEN recruited by the German U-boat service, 28,000 died – a further 5,000 were taken prisoner.

7 ration books

RATIONING BEGAN IN GERMANY in 1939, although Hitler was reluctant to institute it as he was anxious about a negative public reaction. By the end of the war Germans had seven different ration books, colour-coded for different commodities.

227 grams

TO PREVENT FOOD shortages in Britain, the Ministry of Food introduced rationing. German submarines targeted ships importing food to Britain, hoping to starve the nation into defeat. Food rationing began on 8 January 1940, limiting the purchase of certain items. For example, the weekly ration for sugar was 227 grams. People were encouraged to 'dig for victory' by growing their own vegetables.

16 soldiers killed

GERMANY'S INVASION OF DENMARK was the briefest campaign of the war. Denmark was a neutral nation and had a non-aggression treaty with Germany.

THE WAR IN EUROPE SO FAR

Occupying Denmark was a necessary prelude for German plans to invade Norway. Early on 9 April 1940 German troops crossed the Danish frontier and pushed up the Jutland Peninsula. Soldiers were shipped to Copenhagen docks and paratroopers were landed in the first airborne invasion in history. Denmark's military position was untenable. Its government surrendered at 06:00 that day. This saved Denmark from a devastating and bloody defeat. Only sixteen Danish soldiers died during the German invasion.

251 days

NEVILLE CHAMBERLAIN had been Prime Minister since 1937. He had followed a policy of appeasement towards Hitler, not acting when he had united Germany and Austria, and allowing him to annex the Sudetenland Region of Czechoslovakia. He finally declared war in 1939 after Germany invaded Poland. Chamberlain's handling of the war was unpopular. Winston Churchill, a long-term critic of appeasement, serving as First Lord of the Admiralty, gained support as a more effective replacement. On 10 May, after the German invasion of the Low Countries, Chamberlain resigned. He had led Britain for 251 days of World War II. He advised George VI to ask Churchill to form a government, which he duly did. That evening Chamberlain broadcast his resignation address where he asked the nation to 'rally behind our new leader ... and work until this wild beast ... has been finally disarmed and overthrown'.

144 divisions

WHEN THE GERMANS invaded France on 10 May 1940, the Allies had 144 divisions (104 French, twenty-two Belgian, ten British, and eight Dutch). The Germans had slightly fewer (141), but they would prove to be more dynamic and effective. Their *blitzkrieg* ('lightning war') tactics combined tanks and air attacks with infantry to devastating effect. The French defences relied on the Maginot Line, a network of fortifications stretching from the Swiss border to the Belgian frontier. It had numerous concrete pillboxes, bunkers, and dozens of heavy guns. Rather than launch a frontal assault against the Maginot Line, the Germans outflanked it by attacking through the Ardennes Forest and the Low Countries and driving into northern France. The German advance split the Allied forces, forcing the northern part to evacuate from Dunkirk. By the end of May the Low Countries had been defeated and occupied. On 14 June, the German army entered Paris. The French government fell and Marshal Philippe Pétain (a hero of World War I) formed a new government, which almost immediately requested an armistice. The Franco-German armistice was

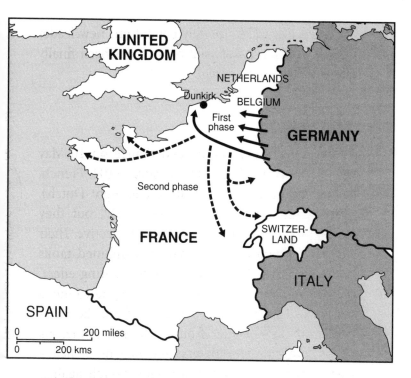

The German Attack Plan, 1940

signed in the town of Compiègne on 22 June. The symbolism was clear. It was the same place that Germany had signed the armistice that had ended World War I. Germany occupied northern France and her coastal areas on the English Channel and Atlantic. The unoccupied *zone libre* formed a Nazi puppet state ruled by Pétain from the spa town of Vichy. Charles de Gaulle, one of the few French generals to have any success against the Germans, had managed to flee to London, where he led the Free French forces who would continue to oppose Hitler.

338,226 soldiers saved

As THE GERMANS ADVANCED through France in May 1940, the commander of the British Expeditionary Force, Viscount Gort, realized evacuation was the only course of action that would prevent complete annihilation. He pulled his troops back to Dunkirk. Before the Germans could fall on the demoralized, disorganized Allied forces trapped at Dunkirk, Hitler ordered them to halt. Why he did this is still a mystery; possibly Göring had persuaded him the Luftwaffe could finish off the Allies or perhaps he believed Britain would not accept surrender if their army had been obliterated. It gave the Allies a chance to flee. The British had cobbled together a fleet of 933 ships. The majority were privately owned ships like yachts, trawlers, and fishing boats. The rescue operation, code-named Dynamo, started on 26 May. German bombing had destroyed Dunkirk's harbour facilities, so the troops had to be picked up from the beaches. With the evacuation under way, Hitler ordered the resumption of the advance on Dunkirk, but their delay had given the Allies time to establish a defensive line. The rescue operation ended on 4 June, with 338,226 British, French, and Belgian troops evacuated. Another 220,000 Allied troops were rescued from other French ports; meaning over half a million had been saved. The Allies had had to abandon their heavy equipment, as well as tons of stores, fuel, and ammunition. In spite of this, Dunkirk was hailed as a miraculous delivery in Britain, and was a major boost to public morale. The British had survived to fight on.

5 years in exile

HAAKON VII HAD BEEN KING OF NORWAY since 1905. A popular figure, Haakon was committed to democracy and played a mostly ceremonial role. Norway, with its long coastline, was an important strategic target. In addition, Germany relied on Swedish iron ore shipments through the Norwegian port of Narvik, which did not freeze over during winter. On 9 April 1940, German troops landed at several points in Norway. Haakon, the royal family, and most of the parliament managed to flee north from Oslo. Germany offered peace if Haakon ordered surrender and appointed Vidkun Quisling, the leader of the Norwegian fascists, prime minister. Haakon refused, but offered to abdicate if the government wished to accept the German demands. They did not, and fighting continued. Allied troops began landing on 14 April to help Norway, but were unable to repel the Germans. On 7 June, Haakon and the royal family left for England. By the next day the last Allied troops had evacuated and on 10 June the remaining Norwegian forces officially capitulated. Apart from the Soviet Union, no other country resisted the German war machine as long as Norway. Hitler called Germany's land campaign 'one of the sauciest undertakings in the history of modern warfare'. However, the German navy sustained heavy losses, preventing them winning maritime superiority over the Allies in the months to come. Haakon spent the rest of the war in England, as figurehead of the Norwegian government-in-exile, returning home in 1945, five years to the day after he had left.

2 sentries killed

THE BRITISH COMMANDOS were a special force set up in June 1940, at Churchill's request, to raid targets in occupied Europe. Their first experience of combat was Operation Collar, a raid on the Pas-de-Calais in northern France. Around 200 Allied soldiers were involved in the operation, which aimed to gather intelligence and damage German equipment. They were transported across the Channel on four Royal Air Force air-sea rescue boats, landing on four beaches early on 24 June. No useful intelligence was found, and nor was any significant damage done to German equipment. There were two brief engagements with German patrols. The only serious casualties came when two unlucky German sentries came across one of the groups on the beach, and were silently killed with bayonets. Despite this unspectacular beginning, the Commandos would go on to play a major role in World War II, and on D-Day.

2,829 people to be arrested

AFTER THE FALL OF FRANCE, Germany switched its attention to invading Britain. The plan, Operation Sea Lion, needed Germany to have dominance of the Channel, both at sea and in the air. On 16 July, Hitler ordered that preparations for the invasion begin. The plan called for three field armies to be transported across the Channel in barges, landing in several places on England's south coast from Lyme Regis to Ramsgate. Once they had landed they would then drive north, encircle London, and advance as far as Northamptonshire. It was then believed Britain would surrender. A detailed plan was drawn up for the German occupation, to be headed by the Nazi official and senior SS officer Dr Franz Six. The British Isles were to be divided into six regional commands, based in London, Birmingham, Newcastle-upon-Tyne, Liverpool, Glasgow, and Dublin. A list of 2,829 people (including Sir Robert Baden-Powell, Winston Churchill, Noël Coward, Charles de Gaulle, and Virginia Woolf) to be immediately arrested was drawn up. The British fascist leader Sir Oswald

Mosley was suggested as a potential leader of a puppet administration. Ultimately, the Luftwaffe was never able to achieve superiority over the Royal Air Force, and the *Kriegsmarine* did not have enough ships to win dominance of the Channel. Given these conditions, Hitler indefinitely postponed Operation Sea Lion on 17 September. When an invasion force did cross the Channel it would be the Allies on D-Day.

20 years old

THE BATTLE OF BRITAIN was a struggle between the Luftwaffe and the Royal Air Force. Lasting from 10 July to 31 October, it was the largest air battle in history. It saw the Allies eventually triumph despite being outnumbered five to one in terms of aircraft and men. German failure to win the Battle of Britain contributed to the postponement of their planned invasion of Britain. The average age of the 3,000 Allied pilots was just twenty years old, and some were as young as eighteen. They were not all British but came from fifteen nations – many from the Commonwealth, but there were also pilots from Poland, Czechoslovakia, Belgium, and Free France. For risking their lives flying fighters at 350 miles per hour, pilot officers were paid a wage of £264 per year. The risk was high; 544 Allied pilots lost their lives during the Battle of Britain. Their sacrifice ensured Britain's safety from a German land invasion.

2 beer barrels

DURING WORLD WAR II, the Spitfire became the symbol of the Royal Air Force's daring and heroism. It had been in service since 1938 and over 20,000 would be built by the time it was retired in 1955. Such was the Spitfire's durability and effectiveness, it was the only airplane in continuous production throughout the war. As an added bonus, Spitfires with under-wing mountings for bombs could also use them to house two beer barrels. After D-Day, the Spitfire's long-range fuel tank was used to carry beer to troops in France. This idea was given an official designation, 'Modification XXX'. If the airplane flew at a high enough altitude, the beer would be nicely chilled on arrival.

57 consecutive nights

STARTING ON 7 SEPTEMBER 1940, the Luftwaffe unleashed a sustained wave of destruction over Britain's cities in what was known as the Blitz. The most heavily targeted city was London, which was bombed for fifty-seven consecutive nights to start the bombing campaign. During this period, an average of 200 bombers flew missions over London every night. The worst night was October 15, when 480 bombers dropped 386 tons of high explosives and 70,000 incendiary bombs. Other strategically important cities, such as Birmingham, Liverpool, and Plymouth, were also targeted. The campaign's aims were threefold. Firstly, it was an attempt to destroy and disrupt Britain's infrastructure and industry. Secondly, it was an act of revenge for the British bombing of Berlin. Finally, it was thought that the bombing campaign would demoralize the British public. The Blitz, which lasted until 20 May 1941, caused a huge amount of damage. More than 43,000 civilians were killed as a result of the bombing and thirty per cent of dwellings in Britain were destroyed or seriously damaged. Despite the mass of bombs dropped, the Blitz did not disable British industrial production, and nor did it seriously damage morale. Indeed, it may have galvanized the British public, uniting them in adversity.

$49,100,000,000

PRESIDENT ROOSEVELT signed the Lend-Lease bill into law on 11 March 1941. It ran until September 1945. The programme saw the United States supply Allied powers with around fifty billion dollars-worth of supplies. Forty nations received supplies under the programme, with Britain, the Soviet Union, China and Free France being the main beneficiaries. When Lend-Lease was started, the United States was not involved in the war, but Roosevelt was determined to support the nations carrying on the fight against the Axis. Britain in particular was running desperately low on cash to purchase supplies and weapons, having already liquidized many of her assets.

Unfortunately, American law prevented Roosevelt from selling weapons on credit or loaning money to nations engaged in war. Roosevelt found a loophole by 'loaning' the Allies material until it was returned or destroyed. In practice little of the material was returned. Roosevelt's promise that the United States would serve as the 'Arsenal of Democracy' against fascism would hold true. American industrial production was vital to Allied survival and eventual victory.

3,343 air raids

MALTA, PART OF THE BRITISH EMPIRE since 1800, occupied a vital strategic position in the Central Mediterranean. Italy entered the war on 10 June 1940 – the next day they bombed Malta. The overstretched Allied forces had been unable to effectively garrison Malta, and it only had a few anti-aircraft guns and a handful of outdated biplanes. Air attacks (over 3,000 raids dropping 15,000 tons of bombs) continued until November 1942, as Malta was a vital base for supplying Allied troops in North Africa. At one point Malta was bombed for 154 consecutive days and nights. During the Siege of Malta, 10,761 buildings were severely damaged or destroyed, but its people never countenanced surrender. On 15 April 1942, George VI awarded Malta the George Cross, the highest civilian honour for gallantry; the medal still features on the Maltese national flag.

3,600,000-strong invasion force

ON 22 JUNE 1941, Germany launched Operation Barbarossa, the invasion of the Soviet Union. The Germans combined with Slovak, Hungarian, Italian, Finnish, and Romanian units to assemble an army of 3.6 million. There were also 3,000 tanks, 7,000 artillery pieces, 750,000 horses, and 2,500 aircraft. It was the largest invasion force gathered in European history. Although Germany and the Soviet Union had signed a non-aggression pact in 1939, Hitler was still determined to overthrow the Communist regime and establish *Lebensraum* ('living space') for Germany in the East. The German High Command believed the Red Army could be quickly defeated and hoped to conquer the European part of Russia by the end of October, before the bitter winter conditions descended. Barbarossa had been originally planned for 15 May, but was delayed for thirty-eight days because of the Axis campaign in the Balkans. Three army groups would push into the Soviet Union: one into northern Russia towards Leningrad (now Saint Petersburg), another through Belarus towards Moscow, and the third through Ukraine towards the vital oil fields in the Caucasus. Between 03.00 and 03.30 the assault was launched by land and by air. No declaration of war was made. The invasion took place on a front stretching 750 miles from the Baltic Sea to the Carpathian Mountains. The element of surprise was total. Despite some warnings, Josef Stalin

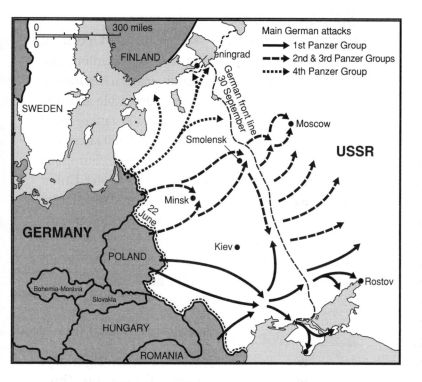

The German Invasion of the USSR, 1941

refused to believe the Germans would attack and no adequate defence plans were in place. Although there were 2.6 million Soviet troops defending the frontier, they quickly fell into disarray as the Axis forces swept east.

50 miles per day

IN THE FIRST WEEKS OF Operation Barbarossa, German panzer (tanks and other armoured combat vehicles) divisions advanced fifty miles per day. Even infantry units, carrying fifty pounds of equipment, were generally able to advance twenty miles every day.

872 days

THE SIEGE OF LENINGRAD (now Saint Petersburg) lasted 872 days, from 8 September 1941 to 27 January 1944. It is the bloodiest siege in history – with over one million soldiers and civilians dying. Hitler had expected the city to 'fall like a leaf'.

3,900 troops

ON 26 JANUARY 1942, 3,900 troops from the Thirty-fourth Infantry Division arrived in Belfast. They were the first American troops to arrive in the United Kingdom. Over 1.5 million more would pass through over the course of the war. The United States had declared war on Japan on 8 December 1941, after their attack on Pearl Harbor. Japan's allies Germany and Italy also declared war on the United States, allowing Roosevelt to pursue a more active involvement in the war in Europe and Africa, as well as Asia.

89 decorations

THE BRETON PORT OF SAINT-NAZAIRE was home to an extensive dry dock. It was the only one on the Atlantic large enough for the biggest German warships. Operation Chariot was a British raid aiming to destroy the dock and harbour facilities. An obsolete Navy destroyer, HMS *Campbeltown*, packed with 4.5 tons of timed explosives, would be driven into the dock sea gates. Commandos would disembark and quell any German resistance. *Campbeltown*, accompanied by two destroyers and sixteen landing boats, left Cornwall on 26 March 1942. At 01:34 on 28 March the *Campbeltown* rammed into the sea-gates. Commandos landed and began destroying the dock's defences and fighting the German soldiers protecting the dock. Once their mission was complete the commandos began to retreat. Many of their landing boats had been destroyed and only one-third returned to England. During the fighting 169 commandos were killed and 215 were captured. Five escaped to Spain and made their way back home. At noon, with forty German officers and civilians on board, the *Campbeltown* exploded, wrecking the dry dock for the duration of the war. Operation Chariot was recognized as 'The Greatest Raid of All'. Eighty-nine decorations were given to the men who fought there, including five Victoria Crosses.

3,642 casualties

ON 19 AUGUST 1942, the Allies launched a raid on Dieppe, code-named Operation Jubilee. The raid would act as a test of the Allied ability to launch a seaborne attack. The troops would hold a perimeter around Dieppe, destroy its defences and harbour facilities, gather intelligence, and withdraw. Nearly 5,000 Canadian troops provided the bulk of the force. One thousand British commandos and fifty US Army Rangers rounded out the Allied numbers. Problems beset the operation. Weather forced its postponement and led to the cancellation of a paratrooper assault. A preliminary aerial bombardment on Dieppe was not undertaken, so as not to inflict casualties on French civilians. The 1,500-strong German garrison in Dieppe was on alert as their agents had warned them of Allied interest in the port. The raid began at 04.50 with largely unsuccessful assaults on coastal batteries. The frontal assault, thirty minutes later, was a total failure. Tanks became bogged down on the beach or held up by concrete obstacles. German machine-gun nests cut down the Allied infantry in a vicious crossfire. At 11.00, with the assault in chaos, the order to retreat was given. Canadian infantry men numbering 3,367 and 275 British commandos were killed, wounded, or captured. German casualties numbered 591. The operation had been a disaster. It did show that any future amphibious operation would need strong preliminary bombardment and close fire support while landing to succeed.

225 confirmed kills

DURING THE BATTLE OF STALINGRAD (now known as Volgograd), the Soviet sniper Vasily Zaytsev recorded at least 225 kills of German soldiers. Amidst the rubble and wreckage of the ruined city, Zaytsev and other Soviet snipers were able to hide and pick off the enemy from a distance. These unseen assassins preyed on the nerves of soldiers far from home locked in an increasingly hopeless situation. The battle for Stalingrad had begun in August 1942, but the Soviets were able to encircle the Axis armies in November. Hitler ordered them to remain in Stalingrad and fight to the death despite their situation being hopeless. The Axis troops ran so low on food that they had to resort to eating rats, sawdust, and wallpaper paste. On 2 February 1943, the exhausted Axis forces in Stalingrad finally surrendered. Just 91,000 survived of over one million men sent to Stalingrad. Soviet casualties were just as heavy – 1.1 million wounded, dead, or captured, as well as 40,000 civilian deaths.

30 degrees Celsius

DURING THE SOVIET COUNTER-OFFENSIVE of winter 1942–3 the temperature dropped to thirty degrees below zero. The Axis troops, who had prepared for a swift campaign, were wholly unprepared for the onset of the savage Russian winter. The majority of

Axis soldiers did not have warm clothing, so many died in their sleep because of the cold. Even the diesel in fuel tanks froze. Much of the Axis army was on the verge of starvation. The Soviet 'scorched earth' policy had made the areas the Axis had advanced to into a barren wasteland. Axis supply lines were dangerously stretched and subject to attack from partisans. Hitler called for 'fanatical resistance' to the Soviet counter-attack, but the tide was turning. November 1942 marked the eastern limit of the Axis offensive into the Soviet Union.

410,000 civilians killed

IN 1942, THE AIR MINISTRY issued the 'Area bombing directive', which allowed Bomber Command to target whole cities rather than specific targets. Next year the Casablanca directive followed, which gave Allied bombers the objective of the 'destruction and dislocation of the German military industrial and economic systems and the undermining of the morale of the German people'. Allied bombing severely restricted and disrupted German industrial production and killed around 410,000 civilians. It led to the diversion of around one million Germans and 55,000 artillery guns to protect Germany from the bombers. Albert Speer called the Allied bombing 'the greatest lost battle on the German side'.

£53 10s 6d

WITH VICTORY IN NORTH AFRICA imminent, the Allies started planning to invade Southern Europe. Sicily was the obvious target. The British instituted Operation Mincemeat to convince the Axis they would not invade Sicily. Royal Navy Intelligence hatched a plan to plant false documents on a corpse and float it to Spain. They hoped its government would allow German Intelligence to examine the corpse and documents. First, the British needed a body. They used a recently deceased thirty-four-year-old Welshman called Glyndwr Michael, with no known living relatives. A false identity was created for him: Captain (Acting Major) William Martin, of the Royal Marines. He was outfitted in uniform, and had a snapshot of his fiancée, 'Pam' (a clerk at MI5). 'Martin' carried a receipt for an engagement ring costing fifty-three pounds, ten shillings, and six pence. Letters from senior military officers were forged suggesting that the Allies planned to invade through Greece and Sardinia. The documents were placed in a briefcase and secured to the corpse. 'Martin' was placed in a canister filled with dry ice to preserve the body. A British submarine transported the canister to the Spanish coast, arriving on 30 April. 'Martin' was fitted with a life jacket and floated ashore. A local fisherman found the body and alerted local authorities. As planned, German Intelligence viewed the documents. Hitler himself was alerted to their contents. He ordered the diversion of troops away from Sicily. Spain handed 'Martin' back to the British, who buried him with full military honours. To complete the ruse, a death notice was posted for 'Martin' in *The Times*.

478,000 men

AFTER NEARLY THREE YEARS of fighting, the Allies won victory over the Axis in North Africa in May 1943. They could now cross the Mediterranean and invade Italy. The first target was Sicily. The invasion, called Operation Husky, would be one of the largest amphibious assaults in history at the time. A total of 478,000 men formed the invasion army. The operation began with a paratrooper assault late on 9 July. Early the next day soldiers were landed by sea on twenty-six beaches spread over the island's southern and eastern coasts. Despite the presence of nearly 300,000 Axis soldiers, the Allies were able to push forward from their landing sites. As a result of the invasion, Benito Mussolini was deposed and imprisoned. By the end of the month Allied victory was a foregone conclusion. The Axis began evacuating men and equipment from the island. The Sicilian campaign ended on 17 August, paving the way for an invasion of the Italian mainland, where the Allies landed on 3 September. Five days later Italy agreed to an armistice with the Allies, who steadily advanced north. Germany, who had thousands of troops in the country, was determined that the

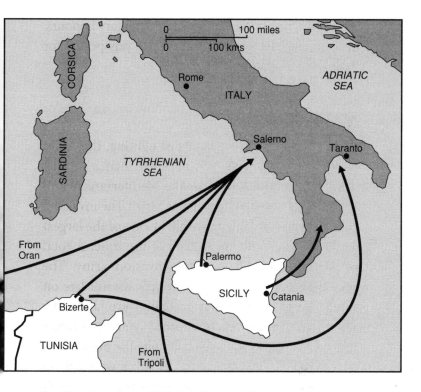

The Allied Invasion of Mainland Italy, 1943

unconquered areas of Italy should fight on. German paratroopers rescued Mussolini and installed him ruler of a Nazi puppet state in northern Italy – the Italian Social Republic. Fighting continued in Italy until May 1945. Mussolini was killed by partisans attempting to escape from the Allies. He was summarily executed and his body was strung up in public.

43

6,300 tanks

THE BATTLE OF KURSK was the largest tank battle in history. In summer 1943, 2,700 German and 3,600 Soviet tanks were involved in a battle fought over an area the size of Wales. Following their defeat at Stalingrad, the Germans needed success. They targeted Kursk in western Russia, where there was a bulge in the Soviet line. The German attack started on 5 July. Every mile gained came at a bloody cost. The Russian defence was ferocious. They had set up trenches, traps, mines, and anti-tank guns and built up a huge reserve force. The Germans never made a decisive breakthrough. After a week of fighting, the Soviets launched a counter-offensive, eventually pushing the Germans back to their start point. On 23 August, the city of Kharkov was liberated, ending the battle. Kursk was the last German offensive in the East.

84,000 messages

AT THEIR PEAK IN 1944 the Allies were decoding 84,000 Enigma-coded messages per month. Poland had made the first breakthrough in 1932, when they had decoded an early version of the Enigma. Their work was a key foundation for the British Code breakers based at Bletchley Park, a mansion set in the Buckinghamshire countryside. On 23 January 1940, they successfully cracked their first German codes. A network of Allied wireless operators (the 'Y' Service) listened in to German radio transmissions, and sent the messages to Bletchley (known as 'Station X') for decoding. One of their Code breakers was a mathematician called Alan Turing. He developed the 'bombe' – an electromechanical device that could be used to work out the settings used by the Enigma machines when the messages were encoded. This meant the coded messages could be deciphered more quickly. German naval communications were deciphered, which allowed the Allies to track U-boats in the Atlantic, meaning shipments from to Britain were more secure. Their work was also key to Montgomery's victory over Rommel in North Africa. The British designated intelligence gained from these decoded message as 'Ultra'. They deceived the Germans into thinking their intelligence breakthroughs had come from secret agents. The Germans continued to use Enigma right until the end of the war, oblivious to the fact the Allies could break their codes. In 1943, the engineer Tommy Flowers designed the world's first electronic computer (the 'Colossus'), which further sped up the code breaking. Both Churchill and Eisenhower agreed that cracking the Enigma code was central to the Allied victory. So well kept was the secret of Enigma that it was not until the 1970s that the story of Bletchley was revealed.

1,727,000 men

THE HOME GUARD, founded as the Local Defence Volunteers in May 1940, was established to help defend Britain in case of a German invasion. It was made up of volunteers who were not eligible for military service (usually because they were too old) and at its peak size it numbered 1,727,000 men. In addition, 31,000 women were involved in the Home Guard. Although never called into action to fight invaders on land, they did the vital job of guarding Britain's coast as well as numerous factories, airfields, and other important areas. In addition, 140,000 Home Guards manned anti-aircraft guns. The organization also helped to prepare youngsters for active service in the military. The Home Guard was disbanded in December 1944.

9,000,000 workers

THE UNITED STATES truly fulfilled Roosevelt's promise to be the 'Arsenal of Democracy'. Almost completely unaffected by enemy attacks, American industry turned out $181,000,000,000 worth of munitions of all kinds during the war. Their shipyards sent out fourteen million tons of shipping. By 1944, nine million workers were employed in the war industry. With so many men posted overseas on military service, the American industrial workforce became increasingly diverse; twenty-nine per cent of them were women and eight per cent were African American.

Chapter 2:
Planning and Preparation

Order number **51**

ON 3 NOVEMBER 1943, Adolf Hitler issued Führer Directive Number 51. It stated, 'the danger in the East remains, but a greater danger now appears in the West; an Anglo-Saxon landing!' This prepared the way for reinforcement of the western front.

86 years old

THE TEHRAN CONFERENCE, held between 28 November and 1 December 1943, was the first meeting in person of all 'Big Three' Allied leaders: Churchill, Roosevelt, and Stalin. Its main result was the Western Allies promising to open up a major second front against the Germans by invading France in May 1944 (delays would push it back to June). At the conference Churchill ceremonially presented Stalin with the magnificent Sword of Stalingrad. This was a double-handed longsword measuring four feet with the inscription: 'To the steel-hearted citizens of Stalingrad, the gift of King George VI, in token of the homage of the British people'. The famed Wilkinson Sword Company had been given the responsibility of manufacturing the blade. Tom Beasley, an eighty-six-year-old who had been making swords since the 1860s, was responsible for forging it. After the conference, the sword returned to the Soviet Union and is now housed in a museum in Volgograd.

1800

SOUTHWICK HOUSE was constructed in 1800, located in the Hampshire countryside north of Portsmouth. From 1940 the Royal Navy had used Southwick to house pupils at their School of Navigation. Once planning for D-Day began, Southwick was selected as the command post of the Supreme Headquarters Allied Expeditionary Force (SHAEF). SHAEF was charged with coordinating and carrying out the Normandy landings. Its supreme commander was the American General Dwight D. Eisenhower. His deputy was Arthur Tedder, who had commanded the Royal Air Force in the Mediterranean Campaign. Commanding land operations for the first phase of the operation would be General Bernard Montgomery, the hero of the North African Campaign. In charge of naval operations was Sir Bertram Ramsay of the Royal Navy.

4 packets of cigarettes per day

IN THE MONTHS BEFORE D-DAY, Eisenhower was smoking four packets of Camel cigarettes per day. This was a stark comparison with the sober Montgomery, who did not smoke or drink.

50 miles

AN INVASION OF Western Europe had been in the pipeline since 1942. Churchill wanted the main drive to be from the Mediterranean into southern Germany, whereas the Americans preferred an invasion from Britain into France. Schemes to invade France in Autumn 1942 and Spring 1943 (code-named Operation Sledgehammer and Roundup, respectively) were both abandoned. Planning for Operation Overlord, the invasion of Normandy, began by June 1943. In charge was Lieutenant-General Frederick Morgan of the British Army, deputized by the American Major General Ray Barker. They decided not to invade through the Calais Region. Although it was the closest part of France to Britain, it was very heavily defended. Instead, they selected Normandy, which was further away but comparatively lightly protected. This would give the invasion a greater element of surprise. Morgan's plan included coordinated landings from sea and by air, as well as the use of artificial harbours. When Montgomery, who would be in command of land operations during the invasion, saw the first drafts of the plan he suggested several changes. He argued that the invasion needed more manpower to succeed and prevent the Germans launching a counter-attack. Montgomery insisted on broadening the invasion front from twenty-five to fifty miles to prevent a bottle-head forming.

17,000,000 maps

IN THE PREPARATION and execution of D-Day around seventeen million different maps were drawn up. They ranged from large-scale strategic maps to detailed local ones. Training maps were labelled with fake names to prevent any intelligence leaks.

70,000 G.I. brides

AMERICAN TROOPS began arriving in the British Isles in 1942. For the most part, they were received warmly across the country, from Bodmin to Glasgow. The American War Department pamphlet, *Instructions for American Servicemen in Britain*, had given the sound advice of not 'showing off', criticizing the coffee, or in any way disparaging the Royal Family. Their comparatively higher wealth and standard of living could cause tension – as did their relations with British women. Girls who were perceived as hanging around with Americans too much were denounced as 'Yankee

Bags'. Nine thousand children were born out of wedlock to American fathers and around 70,000 British women married American servicemen during the war.

£3 15s per month

THE BASIC MONTHLY PAY for a British infantryman with no dependents was three pounds and fifteen shillings. This was by no means a large sum. Unskilled labourers could earn six pounds per month. The wages paid to American soldiers dwarfed both. In the US Army a private had a basic wage of fifty dollars per month, worth just over twelve pounds.

7,000,000 tons of supplies

THE AMERICANS SHIPPED around seven million tons of supplies to the United Kingdom, including 448,000 tons of ammunition. By D-Day the nation had been transformed into what Eisenhower described as 'the greatest operating military base of all time'.

44.8 tons

DURING THE BATTLE OF FRANCE the Germans used the Panzer IV tank to great effect. However, it was outclassed by the Soviet T-34 tank in the East. German engineers examined a captured T-34 to build a tank to match it. They copied its wider wheels and sloping armour, creating the Panzer V Panther. The Panther weighted 44.8 tons, had a top speed of 34 miles per hour, and its main gun had a range of 2,200 yards. Due to shortages of tanks in the East, it was rushed into combat in 1943 and initially suffered from reliability and engine problems. These were overcome and by June 1944 Panthers made up nearly half of German tank strength.

8,000 gallons of fuel

ON AVERAGE, AN AMERICAN TANK would consume 8,000 gallons of fuel every week it was in the field.

8,000 chaplains

BY SUMMER 1944, there were 8,000 American military chaplains on active duty in the United Kingdom representing all major Christian denominations as well as Judaism. Their position was by no means risk-free. During World War II a total of 182 military chaplains died whilst on active service. Four of them (George L. Fox, a Methodist minister, Rabbi Alexander D. Goode, John P. Washington, a Catholic priest, and Clark V. Poling of the Reformed Church in America) died as a result of the sinking of the *Dorchester*, a United States Army Transport ship. On 3 February 1943, the ship was part of a convoy en route to Greenland when it was struck by a torpedo from a

German U-boat. The four chaplains helped to guide men to safety and passed out life jackets. When they ran out, they sacrificed their own life jackets to men who did not have one. All the while, they prayed and sang hymns. Two hundred and thirty of the 904 men on board survived, as the freezing waters meant even those with life jackets succumbed to hypothermia before rescue arrived. The writer Jack Kerouac had previously served on the *Dorchester* and only avoided its final voyage due to being asked to play university American football. The first military chaplain to fall in battle on D-Day was John Reuben Steel, a Methodist minister from Oklahoma who was accompanying the 101st Airborne Division.

10 subsidiary operations

FOR OPERATION OVERLORD to succeed the Allies had to keep the Germans unaware of where and when it would take place. The Germans had fifty-five divisions in France and the Allies only had enough vehicles to transport eight. It was essential the Germans remained ignorant of the invasion site so they could not bring their superior numbers to bear. In early 1944, British intelligence began an ambitious deception plan called Operation Bodyguard. Under the existing Double Cross System, the British had turned many German spies into double agents, and used them to feed false intelligence. These agents would be used in Bodyguard to supply more disinformation. The largest components of Bodyguard were Operations Fortitude North and Fortitude South. They created two phantom armies that were supposedly going to invade Norway and the Calais region, respectively. Operations Graffham and Royal Flush were a series of meetings with neutral Sweden aimed at building ties with her as a prelude to the invasion of Norway. As a result, Germany kept a total of 372,000 men in Norway in preparation for an invasion the Allies had no interest in carrying out. The British also played up the possibility of an invasion around Bordeaux and the Bay of Biscay through Operation Ironside, and used Operation Ferdinand to spread the deception that a major operation in Italy was likely. Operation Vendetta tried to persuade the Germans that the main Allied invasion would come through southern France. To add credence to this, the British carried out another Operation Royal Flush in Spain, aimed at making the Germans believe they were pursuing closer links to the Spanish. Operation Zeppelin was successful in keeping twenty-five divisions of German troops guarding the Balkans and Greece in preparation for an Allied drive into the region from North Africa. Another operation ('Copperhead') saw a Montgomery-lookalike flown to Algeria in May 1944 to make the Germans believe the landings were not imminent.

26 miles per hour

The American medium-sized M4 Sherman tank was the workhorse of the Allied armoured forces. It was designed in 1940 to replace the M3 Lee. The Sherman had superior armour and was able to fully traverse its turret-mounted seventy-five-millimetre gun three hundred and sixty degrees. It could fire armour-piercing rounds or high-explosive ones designed to punch through the armour of other tanks. Added to the turret was a heavy machine gun for anti-aircraft fire along with two other machine guns mounted on the main body of the tank. The British were the first to use the Sherman in battle, at El Alamein, Egypt, in October 1942. The Sherman would supply two-thirds of Britain's armoured strength, as well as being the main American medium tank. The Sherman weighed thirty-four tons and had a top speed of 26 miles per hour. Although its armour and offensive power could not match its German counterpart, the Panther, the Sherman's strength was that it was straightforward to maintain, and performed very reliably. It was relatively inexpensive and quick to build and could be churned out rapidly in large numbers.

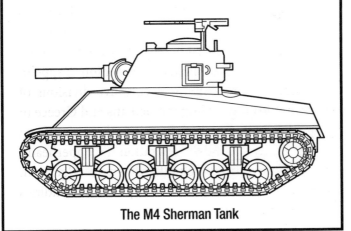

The M4 Sherman Tank

16,500 pigeons

ALLIED WAR PLANNERS were eager to build up knowledge about the German defences and troop positions in occupied Europe as well as local geography. To that end, 16,500 pigeons were fitted with mini-parachutes and released from airplanes over Europe. Each one had a questionnaire attached to its leg. It was hoped that people would fill it in, giving information that might prove useful in planning an attack. Around 2,000 of the pigeons returned to their lofts in the United Kingdom. The French Resistance also used homing pigeons to send intelligence to the Allies. In addition, postcards and holiday snaps of locations in Europe were collected to build up information about local topography and geology. The Germans were so concerned about the threat of these pigeons to security that they commissioned 'Hawk Units' of snipers along the coast to shoot down any pigeons headed for England. Anyone in occupied France in possession of a racing pigeon faced the prospect of court martial or even execution for spying. During the war thirty-two pigeons were awarded the Dickin Medal for animal bravery.

350,000 Resistance fighters

THE FRENCH RESISTANCE fought both the German occupation and the collaborationist Vichy government. The Germans had forced the French to pay for the expense of the occupying forces in their own country, which led to price rises and scarcity of food. The French economy, damaged by the war, further suffered as a result of hundreds of thousands of workers being compulsorily sent to Germany. Resistance fighters conducted a range of activities including spying, helping Allied airmen shot down over France, sabotage, disruption of the economy, propaganda, and assassination of German and collaborationist targets. Men and women from all social and political groups were involved. During its early stages the Resistance was a disparate movement. In May 1943, Jean Moulin unified them under the National Council of the Resistance. This coordinated activity and enabled the Resistance to work more closely with the Allies and the French government in exile. Moulin was arrested the next month and died as a result of brutal interrogation at the hands of the SS. Prior to D-Day there around 350,000 Resistance members in France. They were unlikely to be much direct help during the fighting: only 100,000 of them had serviceable weapons, and just 10,000 had enough ammunition for more than a day of combat. Their main, and most crucial, role was in conducting reconnaissance that gave the Allies vital intelligence about the state of the German defences.

80,000 sub-machine guns

AHEAD OF D-DAY the British parachuted 80,000 sub-machine guns to French Resistance fighters. It was hoped the Resistance would use these weapons, which could fire automatically but were easier to conceal than machine guns, to provide armed support for the Allied invasion forces as well as launch attacks behind German lines. The drops did not go entirely to plan. For example, in Paris only 100 arrived, and Resistance fighters in the city only had 400 weapons in total.

27 fictitious secret agents

JOAN PUJOL GARCIA was a Catalan who had served on both sides during the Spanish Civil War, building up an antipathy to fascism and communism. When World War II started, Pujol decided to spy for Britain as a way to fight fascism. The British rejected his approaches. Undeterred, Pujol decided to work for Germany so the British could later recruit him as a double agent. In 1940, Pujol, posing as a pro-Nazi Spanish functionary able to travel to Britain, approached German Intelligence. They accepted him (giving him the code name 'Arabel') and instructed him to begin recruiting agents in Britain. Instead of going to London, Pujol moved to Lisbon. Despite having never been to Britain, Pujol built up a web of twenty-seven imagined agents using tourist guides, books, newspapers, and newsreels to add detail. The Germans accepted Pujol's reports. He became their top intelligence source for Britain, and was awarded the Iron Cross for his work. In 1942, Pujol made contact with the Americans, who passed him on to MI5. They finally realized Pujol's potential and moved him to Britain that April. He was given the code name 'Garbo'. Pujol continued passing intelligence to the Germans – mostly false or of no military importance. Strategically sensitive material, which built up Pujol's reputation, was always delayed so the Germans would not have time to act on it. Before D-Day Pujol passed hundreds of false messages that were vital in helping to persuade the Germans that the landings would take place around Calais rather than Normandy. Pujol was made a Member of the Most Excellent Order of the British Empire. The Germans never discovered Pujol's deception. In 1949, fearing Nazis would seek revenge, Pujol faked his death in Angola. He moved to Venezuela, where he lived peacefully until he died in 1988.

850,000 troops

COMMANDER-IN-CHIEF of the German Army in the West was Field Marshal Gerd von Rundstedt. A Prussian who had served in the military since 1892, Rundstedt had been sacked from command by Hitler in the aftermath of the German defeat at the Battle of Kiev. In March 1942 Rundstedt was restored to a position of command and took up his post in France. Successive defeats in the East and the need to prepare for invasion in the West meant that by 1944 the resources of the German armed forces were seriously stretched. Rundstedt did not believe the Germans could prevent an Allied landing, but thought they could defeat the invaders by stationing men and armoured units inland ready to counter-attack. Nearly five years of war had greatly decreased the effectiveness of the troops available to Rundstedt. He had 850,000 men at his disposal, but they were of variable quality. Many were convalescing from wounds. Others were teenagers or people previously seen as too old or medically unfit for military service. The latter were grouped into units called 'ear and stomach battalions', so-called because many of them were afflicted with hearing problems or ulcers or distended bellies. Twenty per cent of the German army in the West were *Osttruppen* ('Eastern Troops'). They were conscripts and volunteers from areas of Eastern and Central Europe, such as Poland and Russia, invaded and occupied by the Germans. The Germans initially preferred to use them away from the front line but in France they would be one of the first lines of defence.

7 coastal fortifications

THERE WERE SEVEN heavy coastal batteries between Boulogne and Calais; until the end of 1941 they were the only German fortifications along the French Atlantic coast. After the Saint-Nazaire Raid, Hitler issued Führer Directive Number 40 in March 1942, ordering the construction of a network of coastal defences in the west.

1,200,000 tons of steel and 17,000,000 cubic metres of concrete

THE GERMANS BEGAN constructing the Atlantic Wall to protect occupied Europe from invasion by the Allies in 1942. It was a network of defences that stretched from the Arctic Circle in Norway to the Franco-Spanish border. The Wall was mostly designed and built by the Todt Organization, a group founded in 1938 to carry out large-scale engineering projects, particularly for the military. It was named after its founder, Fritz Todt. After he died in 1942, Albert Speer took over control of the Organization. German civilians were obliged to work for them. As the war went on foreign workers, internees, and prisoners of war were used. These people had little or no choice in joining the Organization and were essentially slave labourers who frequently worked under atrocious conditions building tunnels, bunkers, and artillery batteries. Additionally fortresses were constructed to protect strategically important

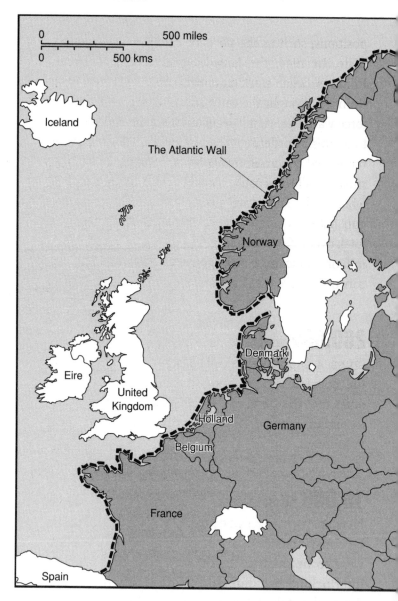

The Atlantic Wall, 1942–1945

positions, such as the ports of Cherbourg and Saint-Malo. In 1944, the famed German general, Erwin Rommel, began work on enhancing the Atlantic Wall. Rommel thought the only way to defeat an invading force was to prevent it securing a beachhead. He tried to do this by ordering the construction of hundreds of reinforced concrete strongpoints along the coast. The smallest pillboxes could contain a machine-gun squad, whereas the largest were big enough to house heavy gun batteries powerful enough to destroy ships. In total, over one million tons of steel and over seventeen million cubic metres of concrete were used in the construction of the Atlantic Wall.

260,000 workers

OVER A QUARTER OF A MILLION MEN worked on the construction of the Atlantic Wall. Of these, only ten per cent were German. The rest were foreigners, forced labourers, prisoners, and a few volunteers.

15,000 strongpoints

HITLER WANTED 15,000 concrete strongpoints to be constructed as part of the Atlantic Wall. They were to be manned by 300,000 men and provide interlocking machine-gun and artillery fire to cut down the Allied landing forces. Hitler designed many of the strongpoints himself. Ultimately the Germans did not have the time, resources, or soldiers to construct and man this many emplacements.

7 pieces of specialized equipment

MAJOR GENERAL PERCY HOBART was a British military engineer who commanded the 79th Armoured Division. This was no conventional unit. Hobart led the development of special modifications designed to meet the challenges of an amphibious landing. These modified vehicles were called 'Hobart's Funnies'. They included armoured bulldozers and ramp carriers to remove obstacles, tanks that could clear mines, 'swimming tanks', and the 'Crocodile' – a tank armed with a long-range flamethrower. The AVRE (Armoured Vehicle, Royal Engineers) was a Churchill tank fitted with seven pieces of equipment. Instead of a tank gun, it had a mortar that launched a forty-pound high-explosive nicknamed the 'flying dustbin'. The AVRE had a mine plough and could unreel a reinforced canvas cloth so it and following vehicles would not sink into the soft sand. It could overcome obstacles by dropping a bundle of poles to fill ditches, deploy a thirty-foot bridge, and was mounted with the 'double onion' – two explosive charges that could be used to destroy fortifications.

30,000 practice launches

THE DEVELOPMENT of a reliable 'swimming tank' was a major aim for the Allies, who hoped to use them in the invasion of Normandy. They would be carried close to shore in landing craft and then launched near to the coastline, where they would be able to provide immediate support to infantry once they came ashore. In 1940, Nicholas Straussler, a Hungarian-born engineer working for the British, had the concept of creating a collapsible canvas screen that would be attached around the tank's hull. When inflated, it made the tank buoyant enough to float. Rear-mounted propellers were added, enabling the tank to actually 'swim' forward. Tanks with these devices became known as 'Duplex Drives' (or DD tanks – leading to their nickname 'Donald Duck tanks'). The largest tanks were simply too heavy for the device to operate, but it was ideal for the medium-sized Sherman tank. It took fifteen minutes to deploy the screen and once in the water DD tanks could swim at over four miles per hour. Around 30,000 practice launches were undertaken by swimming tanks during the preparation for D-Day.

30,000 Spanish Communists

AFTER GENERAL FRANCO's fascists won victory (with Nazi assistance) in the Spanish Civil War in 1939, thousands of Republicans fled to France. Their escape from fascism was brief. The German occupying forces conscripted 30,000 Spanish Communists as forced labourers during the construction of the Atlantic Wall. Many of these Spanish refugees would also join the French Resistance.

23 feet thick

THE LARGEST GERMAN coastal batteries were protected by concrete twenty-three feet thick. They housed sixteen-inch artillery pieces stationed to blow ships out of the water. The most impressive fortifications were in the Calais Region, constructed as part of the preparations for Operation Sea Lion, and strengthened because the Germans expected the invasion there.

319 aircraft

IN THE MONTHS BEFORE D-DAY the American Eighth Air Force, augmented by the Royal Air Force and the Ninth Air Force, pulverized the infrastructure of the German occupying army in France. Their raids targeted railways, airfields, and bridges in a concerted effort to limit German ability to move troops and materiel. The Allied air campaign also decimated the Luftwaffe's offensive capability. By the time of the landings the German air commander in Western Europe, Field Marshal Hugo Sperrle, was left with just 319 serviceable aircraft, leaving the Luftwaffe outnumbered over thirty-to-one. These successes came at a great cost for the Allies – between 1 April and 5 June the Allies lost 12,000 aircrew and 2,000 aircraft.

18,000 workers

ALLIED BOMBING RAIDS on the French railway network had thrown the country's infrastructure into chaos. Eighteen thousand workers labouring on the Atlantic Wall had to be withdrawn from their tasks to maintain and repair France's damaged railways, and keep trains running. This slowed down the construction of Germany's coastal defences.

0 soldiers

THE FIRST US ARMY GROUP ('FUSAG') was a phantom military formation, supposedly made up of 150,000 men. Despite having no actual soldiers, it still played a vital role in the run-up to D-Day. FUSAG existed only on paper, and was supposedly stationed in Dover. This was to make the Germans believe there were plans to land troops in the Calais region. Allied double agents, in concert with props, decoys, and false radio signals, successfully persuaded the Germans that FUSAG existed. To help the deception, George S. Patton was appointed the commander of FUSAG. Patton had been a highly successful commander in North Africa and Italy, and was greatly respected by the Germans. Patton had fallen out of favour with Eisenhower for slapping two soldiers suffering from battle fatigue in August 1943 and had been removed from combat command. As a result of the scandal, General Omar N. Bradley had been given the task of leading the American land forces at D-Day instead of Patton. The Germans were so convinced of the existence of FUSAG that even after the landings at Normandy, they kept men around Calais believing a landing there was imminent. Patton returned to combat duties after D-Day as the commander of the US Third Army, which he led through France and into Germany.

200 miles per hour

TWO HUNDRED MILES PER HOUR was the usual cruising speed of Allied heavy bombers such as the Avro Lancaster, the Handley Page Halifax, the Boeing B-17 Flying Fortress, and the Consolidated B-24 Liberator. They all had ranges of around 2,000 miles and could carry bomb payloads of 6,000 pounds.

7,000,000 jerry cans

BETWEEN JANUARY AND JUNE 1944, British factories produced seven million jerry cans in preparation for the invasion of France. These portable containers were made from steel lined with plastic to prevent leakage. Their main use was to carry fuel. They had three handles on top, enabling them to be carried by one or two people. Two empty cans could be carried in one hand. Supply of petrol was crucial in mechanized warfare and jerry cans allowed it to be more easily distributed. Jerry cans originated in Germany ('Jerry' being the slang for Germans) in 1937, and had been used with great success in the early years of the war. They were so superior to Allied fuel containers that captured German jerry cans were often used in preference to domestic designs, which were unwieldy and prone to leakage. The Allies began to make their own jerry cans, based on the German design. They had a laden weight of sixty pounds and were eighteen inches tall, thirteen inches wide, and seven inches deep. They could hold five gallons of petrol when filled. Roosevelt stated that, 'without these cans it would have been impossible for our armies to cut their way across France'.

8,000 tons of fuel per day

AN EFFECTIVE FUEL SUPPLY was essential to Allied plans for the invasion of France. Transferring the oil across the Channel using tankers was rejected as bad weather and U-boat attacks could disrupt shipping. 'Ship to shore' pipelines would disrupt operations on the landing beaches. Arthur Hartley, the chief engineer of the Anglo-Iranian Oil Company, developed the idea of delivering the fuel using a pipeline under the Channel using modified underwater telegraph cables. Testing for the project, code-named 'Pluto' (Pipeline Under The Ocean), began in 1942. The pipes had to be flexible yet resistant to water pressure. Pluto used two types of pipe; a flexible one with a seventy-five millimetre diameter lead core and a more rigid steel pipe. The system stood up to the harshest weather conditions, and could pump up to 8,000 tons of fuel per day. Oil terminals, mainly around Liverpool and Bristol, were constructed in areas of the country out of reach of Luftwaffe raids. They were then piped to Sandown in the Isle of Wight, where they would be sent onto Europe. The pumping stations were disguised as bungalows, gravel-pits, garages, barns, and even ice cream shops to maintain the operation's secrecy. In total, the pipeline weighed fifty-five tons per nautical mile.

30-mile sections

THE STEEL PIPES used in Operation Pluto were welded into runs of thirty miles in length in preparation for being laid. They were then wound around ninety-feet-long steel drums, which looked like giant floating cotton reels. They were known as 'Conundrums'. Three tugboats were tethered to the Conundrums. As they travelled forward, the Conundrum would unwind, uncoiling the steel pipe. When fully loaded, the Conundrums weighed 1,600 tons.

2,500 pounds

THE AMERICAN REPUBLIC P-47 Thunderbolt could carry a payload of bombs weighing 2,500 pounds. In addition, it was armed with ten rockets. The Thunderbolt was used as a long-range escort in bombing raids, as well as a fighter-bomber, and played a major part in winning Allied air superiority over France.

3.1 tons and **29** men

THE GERMANS WERE THE FIRST to use military gliders in combat during the Battle of France in 1940. Gliders were engineless aircraft towed into the air by larger, powered airplanes. When they approached their target zone the gliders were released from the towline and then piloted to a landing site. Gliders were designed to be used only once, so they were mostly made from light, inexpensive wood. As they had no engines they moved in near-silence. The main British glider was the Airspeed AS.51 Horsa (named after an Anglo-Saxon warrior who had conquered parts of Britain). It went into production in 1942, and could carry over three tons of equipment and twenty-nine troops. The Horsa was used to transport jeeps and light artillery. It was first used in combat on a 1942 raid on a chemical plant in Norway. It was producing 'heavy water', an essential component of nuclear weapons and reactors that the Germans were developing. The British planned to use two Horsas to land troops, who would destroy the plant and disrupt the German nuclear programme. The raid was a disaster. Both Horsas and one of the towing-craft crashed, killing many aboard. The rest were captured and summarily executed. Horsas were used more successfully during the Italian campaign, giving the Allied war planners the confidence to give them a major role in the D-Day Landings. The Horsa was larger than its American counterpart, the Waco CG-4A, which could carry up to fifteen men or 1.7 tons.

80 millimetres of armour

THE BAZOOKA was an American portable shoulder-mounted rocket launcher, shaped like a tube. It was developed by the military engineer Edward Uhl. He was charged with finding a way for infantry units to launch explosive grenades. In 1942, Uhl saw a metal tube in a scrap pile, giving him the idea for the weapon. Its official designation was the M1 rocket launcher and it was introduced into combat in late 1942. Soldiers nicknamed it the 'Bazooka' after a simple brass instrument made of pipes, invented by the comedian Bob Burns in the 1930s. The Bazooka could fire a 3.4-pound charge at a range of 250 yards, and penetrate up to 80 millimetres of armour. Despite being developed primarily as an anti-tank weapon, the Bazooka was equally useful when used to destroy bunkers, machine-gun nests, and other fortifications. The Germans copied the design of the Bazooka to produce their own anti-tank rocket launcher, which they called the *Panzerschreck* ('tank frightener').

4 metres high

ROMMEL AIMED TO DISRUPT Allied paratroop and glider operations by placing obstacles in open areas likely to be used as landing sites. His idea was drive millions of wooden poles, around four metres high, into the ground. Barbed wire and mines connected to tripwires were hung between the poles. Every third pole was mounted with an explosive device. The poles became known as *Rommelspargel* ('Rommel's asparagus'). To further disrupt landings, many areas were permanently flooded. Despite so many poles being used, the system did little to disrupt the landing of Allied troops from the air.

4,000,000 mines

FOUR MILLION MINES littered the beaches and waters at Normandy. Some were large mines with enough power to destroy or incapacitate landing craft, tanks, and other vehicles. Others, like the S-mine, were designed to kill or maim soldiers. The Americans nicknamed the S-mine 'Bouncing Betty', because when triggered by pressure or a tripwire, it fired into the air and then detonated at waist height. When it exploded it sprayed a devastating wave of shrapnel. In addition to the mines, the Germans placed around half a million obstacles, such as bundles of barbed wire, logs topped with mines, and ten-foot-high steel gates, at Normandy to slow down soldiers attempting to make their way across the beach.

200 grams of TNT

THE GERMAN SCHUHMINE 42 was packed with a 200-gram block of explosive TNT, contained in a hinged wooden box. When pressure was applied to the top of the box, it set off the mine. As it was mainly made of wood it was cheap to produce and very difficult to locate with metal detectors.

200,000 newspapers dropped

SEFTON DELMER was a British journalist born in Germany to Australian parents. Fluent in German, he wrote for the *Daily Express* and was the first British journalist to interview Hitler. During the war Delmer worked for the Political Warfare Executive, a British government organization set up to distribute propaganda in enemy territory. Delmer helped start several clandestine radio stations that broadcast a mixture of music, news, and reports aimed at demoralizing the German people and military. In 1943, Delmer had the idea of creating a double-sided news-sheet aimed at German soldiers, with the title, *Nachrichten für die Truppe* ('News for the Troops'). Delmer described its general line as: 'The war is lost: better chuck out Hitler now rather than later'. The project was approved and Delmer was given a team of twenty-five writers and editors. The first edition was prepared on 25 April 1944, but numbered 'nine', to confuse authorities into thinking they had missed earlier editions. It contained news of the devastating bombing of Germany and the success of the Allied armies. Aircraft dropped 200,000 copies of the first edition of the newspaper, but over as wide an area as possible to ensure that the invasion area remained a secret. On D-Day one million copies were dropped, reporting the breach of the Atlantic Wall. *Nachrichten für die Truppe* remained in circulation until the war ended in Europe.

7,815,360 pounds of soap

IT WAS ESTIMATED THAT the Allied invasion forces would require nearly eight million pounds of soap for their first four months in France.

946 dead

THE GRAVELLY BEACHES of Slapton Sands, on the Devon coast, were an ideal place for rehearsals for the landings in Normandy. One such rehearsal was 'Exercise Tiger'. Troops were to disembark from landing craft under fire from live ammunition. The practice landings began on the morning of 27 April. Due to delays, miscommunication, and confusion, friendly fire killed several soldiers. Precise numbers who died during the incident are still undetermined. That evening another convoy of landing craft made its way to Slapton. They had only one armed escort, instead of the planned two, as one of the ships was in port undergoing repairs. The under-protected landing craft were spotted by a patrol squadron of nine German E-boats (a fast attack craft also known as the *Schnellboot*) near Lyme Bay. Early on 28 April, they fired torpedoes, hitting three of the landing craft. One managed to limp ashore; the other two sank. Another landing craft was damaged by friendly fire. In the chaos, there was little time to launch lifeboats. Many drowned or died of hypothermia floating in the cold water. In total, 946

American soldiers and sailors died that night. It was a major embarrassment and survivors were sworn to secrecy. The disaster also threatened the D-Day landings themselves. There were ten missing officers who had detailed knowledge about the invasion of Normandy. It was feared they might have been picked up by the Germans, scuppering the security of the D-Day plans. The bodies of the ten officers were recovered and Operation Overlord would go ahead as planned.

Gale Force **6**

THE FAILURE OF THE DIEPPE RAID in 1942 had shown the difficulty of capturing a heavily protected port such as Cherbourg. The solution was to create a prefabricated harbour that could be towed across the Channel and then assembled. Various prototypes were tested in the waters off south-west Scotland. They could stand up to Gale Force Six winds of up to forty-nine miles per hour. The harbours were given the code name 'Mulberry'.

'1 of the USA'

APPEARED AS A CLUE IN THE *Daily Telegraph* crossword on 3 May 1944. The solution was 'Utah', the code name of one of the landing beaches assigned to the Americans on D-Day. The names of other beaches, 'Juno', 'Gold', and 'Sword', had appeared over the previous weeks. 'Omaha', 'Overlord', 'Mulberry', and 'Neptune' would follow. The appearance of so many words associated with the top-secret D-Day Landings worried the Allied intelligence agencies. Was there a German mole leaking secrets via the medium of puzzles? MI5 sent two officers to interview the compiler of the crosswords, a teacher called Leonard Dawe, who had been compiling crosswords for the *Telegraph* since 1925. He was the headmaster of the Strand School, which had been evacuated from London to Effingham in Surrey. According to Dawe, the MI5 officers 'turned me inside out' to find an explanation for the appearance of the words. Eventually, it was determined there was no leak, and that the presence of the words was a coincidence. Dawe continued to set crosswords until his death in 1963. After the war an explanation emerged. Sometimes Dawe compiled crosswords by asking his pupils to fill in words into a blank grid. Effingham was located close to camps where American and Canadian soldiers waiting for D-Day were stationed. Seemingly, the students of the Strand School had heard these code words being mentioned by soldiers and entered them into the grid, unwittingly sparking off a panic in the Allied intelligence services.

Pittsburgh Pirates **7**, New York Giants **6**

THREE DAYS BEFORE D-DAY there was a potentially disastrous security breach. A Teletype operator called Joan Ellis, working for the Associated Press, was practising typing out the message to be sent out when the Normandy landings took place. Unbeknownst to her she was actually connected to the global Telex system and her news flash was sent to press rooms across five continents. It read: 'URGENT PRESS ASSOCIATED NYK FLASH: EISENHOWER'S HQ ANNOUNCES ALLIED LANDINGS IN FRANCE'. Associated Press managed to deny the dispatch twenty-three minutes later, and the announcement did not appear in any newspapers or news reports. Before they did this, the invasion was announced at a baseball match played at the Polo Grounds in Upper Manhattan, New York City. Thousands of spectators watching the New York Giants lose narrowly to the Pittsburgh Pirates were told the invasion had taken place, and asked to offer silent prayer for the soldiers taking part. The news flash was also read out at a horse-racing meeting at Belmont Park in nearby Long Island.

Chapter 3:
Order of Battle and the Crossing

500-feet cloud base

THE NORMANDY LANDINGS needed favourable weather to succeed. Eisenhower had selected 5 June (the day before a full moon, which would provide natural illumination) for the landings. May had been a pleasant month. When June came the weather began to change for the worse. Three different teams (from the Royal Navy, the Met Office, and the US Army Air Forces) were charged with forecasting the weather. Captain James Martin Stagg, a Royal Air Force officer, had the task of presenting their findings to Eisenhower. Unfortunately the three teams seldom agreed. The Americans thought 5 June would be suitable whilst the two British teams predicted high winds that would threaten the safety of the sea crossing and overcast conditions that would lead to a cloud base (lowest visible point of cloud) of 500 feet, which would disrupt air operations. Stagg took the majority opinion. As a result, on 4 June, Eisenhower put the operation on hold. Thousands of men who had already boarded landing craft had to remain in port on their ships. At a meeting at 4.30 a.m. on 5 June, Stagg told Eisenhower that the weather would briefly improve the next day. This was the window the Allies needed; Eisenhower ordered the landings to go ahead. Allied ships began leaving port at nine in the morning, aiming to land in France early on 6 June.

92 radar sites

THE GERMANS HAD NINETY-TWO manned radar (or, as it was known in German, *Funkmessgerät* – 'radio measuring device') stations as part of their Atlantic Wall in northern France and Belgium. These systems used radio waves (and later, microwaves) to locate the position of enemy shipping and aircraft, and provide an early warning of their presence. During World War II radar equipment had become increasingly sophisticated and accurate (although the British and Americans had gained the technological upper hand over the Germans in this area). Radar had been essential to Allied victory in the Battle of Britain in 1940, enabling them to locate German aircraft. Accordingly, eliminating enemy radar brought with it major tactical advantages. On D-Day the Allies were keen to destroy any German radar sites that might detect their movements. They used three mobile devices, called 'Ping Pongs', to detect the German radar systems and give their bearings. Allied Mosquitos, Spitfires, and Typhoons would fly 2,000 sorties against German radar stations. By the evening of 7 June only sixteen had not been attacked, and none were fully operational in the invasion area.

15-second intervals

OPERATIONS 'TAXABLE' and 'Glimmer' were part of the ongoing British attempt to draw the Germans forces away from the invasion beaches at Normandy by tricking them into believing the main landings would take place elsewhere. Taxable was focused on the area between Le Havre and Dieppe whilst Glimmer targeted the Calais Region. Early on D-Day a force of Royal Air Force bombers would drop tons of aluminium strips, called 'chaff'. This would appear as an invasion fleet on German radar. Operation Taxable was tasked to 617 Squadron, known as the 'Dambusters' for their daring 1943 raid on German dams in the Ruhr using the bouncing bomb. Glimmer was carried out by 218 Squadron. Both operations followed a similar pattern. Once the aircraft reached the English coast they flew over the Channel at 180 miles per hour in a line with two miles between each plane, dropping chaff at fifteen-second intervals. After 150 seconds they turned 180 degrees and flew on a parallel course for 130 seconds and then repeated the process. Essentially they were flying in a circuit that was edging steadily towards France. The chaff created the illusion of a fleet moving towards the French coast. This precise manoeuvre was carried out in darkness. To add to the deception, underneath the bombers were several boats towing radar-reflecting balloons and transmitting false radio traffic of a large fleet. Glimmer was the more successful operation. The Germans actually sent planes to scout out the 'fleet' and their coastal batteries fired on its position.

4 Harbour Defence Motor Launches

THE ALLIES FURTHER ATTEMPTED to disrupt the German defence effort by sending out a 'radio countermeasure' force on the western flank of the invasion fleet. This operation, code-named 'Big Drum', aimed to jam German radar stations around Cherbourg, on the Cotentin Peninsula. It was hoped the Germans would send forces to investigate the jamming. A group of four HDMLs, led by Lieutenant Commander H.M. Nees, approached their target early on D-Day and began operations, eventually closing to one and a half miles from the coast.

The Germans did not respond to the diversion and the convoy returned home, with all four HDMLs arriving safely in the Sussex port of Newhaven.

6,939 ships

THE PROCESS OF SHIPPING the invasion force across the Channel on D-Day was called Operation Neptune. Overseeing this vast effort was Admiral Sir Bertram Ramsay, who had been responsible for leading the evacuations from Dunkirk. As a result of Allied air operations and poor weather the Luftwaffe would not provide much of a threat to the invasion fleet. Allied deception plans had convinced Hitler the actual landing would take place around Calais, drawing resources away from Normandy. Nearly seven thousand ships would be used in the largest seaborne invasion of all time. Over 150,000 men, mostly from infantry divisions (ID), crossed the Channel on D-Day, boarding at various points from Cornwall to the Thames Estuary. They journeyed to their ships from assembly areas located across southern England. Troops were sealed in these areas (called 'sausages' because of the shape they appeared as on maps) living in tents and huts in the days before the invasion so that no security leaks would occur. Craft at Portsmouth Harbour were so tightly packed together one could walk ashore without touching the water. The assembly area for the fleet

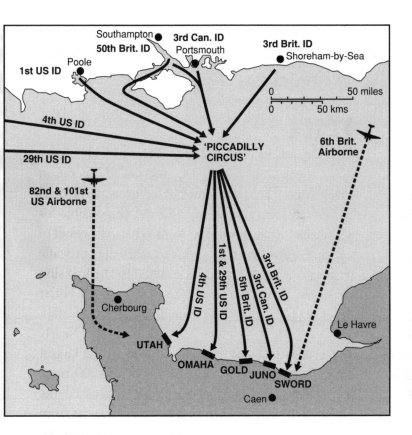

The D-Day Invasion Plan, 1944

just off the Isle of Wight on the South Coast was aptly called 'Piccadilly Circus'. Leading the armada were 277 mine sweepers to detect explosive devices in the water. Following them were 138 large warships that would bombard the German defences from the sea. Behind them came the hundreds of ships and boats (including 864 merchant vessels redeployed for military use) carrying the men, vehicles, and supplies.

17 hours

THE CROSSING TOOK SEVENTEEN HOURS; rough seas meant many soldiers suffered from severe seasickness. To compound this, prior to D-Day American soldiers had been issued with new wool uniforms coated with a thick paste to prevent German poison gas (which was never used) penetrating the fabric. This made their clothes stiff, greasy, and foul-smelling.

8 nations

THE ROYAL, CANADIAN, and US Navies provided the bulk of the craft and personnel used during Operation Neptune. Ships and men from five other nations also took part. In total 195,700 men were assigned: around sixty per cent were British, over twenty-five per cent were American, and the rest were from other Allied countries. The Free French Navy supplied ten ships, the Poles two cruisers, the Norwegians three destroyers, the Dutch two sloops (single-mast sailing boats), and the Greeks two ships that escorted convoys to landing beaches.

3 ships

AFTER NEARLY FIVE YEARS of naval warfare, by June 1944 the *Kriegsmarine* had only three ships larger than destroyers (fast, mid-sized escort vessels) still available for service. They were three cruisers; the *Prinz Eugen*, the *Nürnberg*, and the *Emden* (which had been in service for nearly twenty years). None were at sea to oppose the Allied crossing on D-Day.

1909

THE OLDEST BATTLESHIP in action on D-Day (and on active service in the entire US Navy) was the USS *Arkansas*. Congress had authorized its construction in 1909. The *Arkansas* was commissioned in 1912, and served during World War I. By 1941 she was on the verge of being scrapped, but was reprised when the United States entered the war. The *Arkansas* was used as an escort vessel for convoys in the Atlantic. On D-Day her task was to bombard the German batteries at Cherbourg with her twelve, twelve-inch guns. After D-Day the *Arkansas* operated in the Mediterranean and the Pacific. She met her end in 1946 when she was selected as one of the test subjects for the impact of nuclear weapons on ships at Bikini Atoll. After surviving two world wars and an airborne atomic blast, the *Arkansas* was sunk by a submerged nuclear detonation on 25 July 1946. In terms of age, the *Arkansas* was by no means atypical of the battleships serving on D-Day; others included the USS *Texas*, HMS *Warspite*, the USS *Nevada*, and HMS *Ramillies* (commissioned in 1914, 1915, 1916, and 1917, respectively). These venerable craft were nicknamed 'the old ladies'.

5,000 pounds

THE DUKW WAS A SIX-WHEELED American amphibious truck that was capable of carrying 5,000 pounds in depths of up to fifteen feet. The 'Duck', as it was also known, was designed by a partnership of the famed New York yacht designers Sparkman and Stephens and the General Motors Corporation. Its name came from its manufacturing code: 'D' denoted it was designed in 1942, 'U' that it was a utility vehicle, 'K' that it had front-wheel drive, and 'W' that it had two powered rear axles. On D-Day the DUKW was mostly used to ferry troops and supplies ashore from transport ships on the coast.

4,126 landing craft

OVER FOUR THOUSAND landing craft were used to transport the invasion army to the Normandy beaches.

20 tanks

THE ALLIES WOULD NOT have immediate access to harbour facilities on D-Day, so the LST Mk. 2 (Landing Ship, Tank) would play a vital role in bringing heavy equipment to shore. It could carry twenty tanks, 400 fully equipped soldiers, or 2,100 tons of supplies, and also would be used as a hospital ship. Designed by a joint Anglo-American team, its bow doors opened to around four metres, meaning that when the LST came ashore vehicles could drive straight out onto the shore. They entered action during the 1942 landings in North Africa and were also heavily used during the Italian and Pacific Campaigns. Over one thousand LSTs were produced during the war, and 229 were used on D-Day. Despite being nicknamed 'Large, Slow Targets', they were sturdy ships capable of taking a large amount of enemy fire.

37 lines cut

FRANCE'S STATE RAILWAY NETWORK, the SNCF (*Société Nationale des Chemins de fer Français*), was crucial to the success of the German occupation and military presence. In 1943, French railway workers formed the Résistance-Fer, which sabotaged the railway system and informed the Allies of German troop movements. They played a vital part in the success of D-Day. Once the Allied landings took place, the Germans could quickly deploy reinforcements by train. To stall this, in the days before D-Day, the Résistance-Fer cut thirty-seven railway lines in Burgundy and eastern France. This was part of 'Plan Vert', a coordinated operation with the Resistance to sabotage the railways. This thoroughly disrupted German plans and meant they had to send reinforcements by road, which was considerably slower. Resistance fighters also destroyed electrical stations, cut communications cables, and tried to disrupt German reinforcements sent to Normandy.

1 pound

EACH AMERICAN general infantryman was issued with a helmet that weighed one pound. Aside from protecting the head, it could be used as a wash basin, cooking cauldron, digging tool, and even a weapon in dire situations.

5,500,000 rifles

THE M1 GARAND was the standard-issue rifle of the American Army from 1936 to 1957. It was named after its designer, John C. Garand. Unlike bolt-action rifles, where bullets had to be chambered manually between shots using a small handle, the Garand was semi-automatic. It was loaded with a 'clip' of eight cartridges. Each time it was fired the spent cartridge was ejected and a new cartridge was chambered ready to be fired when the trigger was pulled. When the clip was used up, it was automatically ejected. As a result the Garand could be fired at over three times the rate of bolt-action weapons. During the war the United States produced over five million Garands. It was known for its accuracy, sturdiness, and reliability in all conditions. Patton lauded it as 'the greatest single battle implement ever devised by man'. The majority of British and Canadian soldiers at D-Day used the Lee Enfield, a bolt-action rifle that was still capable of firing up to thirty aimed rounds per minute.

$900 per jeep

THE JEEP WAS THE WORKHORSE of the Allied landing forces. It was designed by Willys-Overland to fulfil the US Army's need for a small, reliable, all-purpose, reconnaissance vehicle capable of traversing all terrains. Both Willys-Overland and Ford produced the vehicle to meet demand. Known as the 'GP' (general purpose), this became contracted to 'jeep'. Around 650,000 of them were produced during the war (about one-third went to the British and the Soviets) at a cost of $900 by 1945. Its uses were myriad; from a mobile weapon platform (a machine gun could be mounted on a swivel instead of a backseat) to a medical evacuation vehicle. The jeep's four-wheel drive, handling and reliability over all surfaces, quarter-ton carrying capacity, and top speed of sixty-five miles per hour, made it a favourite of the Allies in all theatres of the war. The famed American war correspondent Ernie Pyle called the jeep 'faithful as a dog, as strong as a mule, and as agile as a goat'.

15,766 aircraft available

ON THE EVE OF D-DAY, an air armada of unprecedented size had been assembled in Britain. The Allies had been building up the force for months. It would bomb German targets and defences and transport men and supplies to France. It included 5,049 fighters, 3,467 heavy bombers, 1,645 light and medium bombers, 2,316 transports, 2,591 gliders, and 698 aircraft of other types. Each one was painted with bold black and white 'invasion stripes' on its wings so they could be easily identified and not be mistaken for German aircraft. They would face just 815 German aircraft.

13,348 paratroopers

THE ASSAULT ON NORMANDY would begin with the landing of 13,348 paratroopers (mostly from the US Eighty-Second and 101st Airborne divisions)

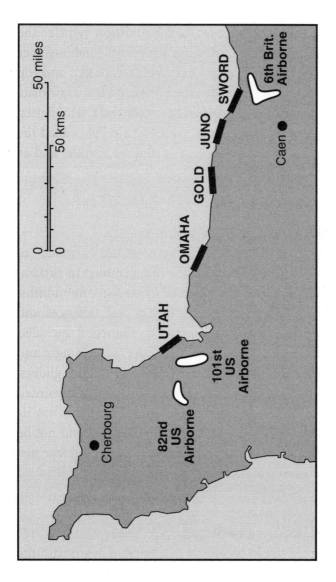

D-Day Parachute Landing Sites, 1944

five hours before the coastal landings. Just after 10 p.m. on 5 June, 925 C-47s took off from airfields in England to drop them behind enemy lines in Normandy. They would be reinforced later on D-Day by the arrival of 4,000 men in 500 gliders.

18 paratroopers

IN 1936, THE DOUGLAS AIRCRAFT COMPANY introduced the DC-3 as a civilian airliner. Powered by two 1,200 horsepower propellers capable of reaching a maximum speed of 224 miles per hour, the DC-3 could fly across the continental United States in just fifteen hours. When the United States entered the war, the American armed forces adapted the DC-3 for military service. Renamed the C-47 Skytrain, it became their primary transport aircraft and was heavily used by the other Allies (it was known as the 'Dakota' in the Royal Air Force). The C-47 was essentially a modified SC-3 with a reinforced floor and a large rear cargo door. It could carry 6,000 pounds of cargo or twenty-eight armed men and was large enough to hold a fully assembled jeep, as well as be modified to tow gliders. If used for medical purposes, it could hold fourteen patients on stretchers and three nurses. On D-Day, the C-47 was mostly used to drop paratroopers. Each one could hold a 'stick' of eighteen paratroopers.

4 Hershey chocolate bars

INCLUDING THEIR PARACHUTE, American paratroopers carried up to 120 pounds of equipment. Their standard gear included a Garand rifle, additional ammunition, hand grenades, a .45 calibre Colt automatic pistol, a trench knife, flares, medical kit, torch, and a pocket compass. In each twelve-man squad of paratroopers one man also carried a light machine gun. Officers carried additional equipment including a sub-machine gun and plastic explosives. As it was uncertain when they would be resupplied, they carried a cooking kit, food for three days, and an emergency ration pack. This contained chewing gum, bouillon cubes, Nescafe instant coffee, four chocolate bars, a package of hard candy, tobacco, and water purification tablets. Their equipment also included twenty-four sheets of toilet paper.

2 syrettes

AMERICAN PARATROOPERS carried two morphine syrettes (disposable hypodermic injectors similar to a syringe but with a collapsible tube rather than a rigid one) in their equipment packs; 'one for pain, two for eternity'.

2,478 Bronze Stars

ON D-DAY, THE EIGHTY-SECOND DIVISION would be dropped around the town of Sainte Mère Église, behind Utah Beach. This would actually be their second experience of combat in France. When the Eighty-Second was formed as an infantry division in 1917 to fight in World War I, it featured men from all forty-eight states (Alaska and Hawaii did not become states until 1959). Hence it was given the nickname 'All American' and its distinctive red, white and blue 'AA' shoulder patch. In 1942, the Eighty-Second was reactivated as a combat unit. Under the command of Major-General Matthew B. Ridgway the division was transformed from an infantry unit to the first airborne division in the US Army. Its training base at Fort Bragg, North Carolina, became famed as the 'Home of the Airborne'. By 1943 the complex had 1,750

US Airborne
Shoulder
Patches

buildings and was home to over 100,000 personnel. Ironically, when the Eighty-Second first entered battle in Morocco in May 1943, they landed by boat. Most of the division was moved to the United Kingdom during early 1944 to prepare for D-Day. By then they had lost 533 men killed in action and 2,749 wounded. During the war the 'All Americans' won a total of 2,478 Bronze Stars for heroism in combat, the fourth-highest individual award in the American military.

214 days in combat

D-DAY WOULD BE THE 101st Airborne Division's (the 'Screaming Eagles') first taste of combat. Their mission was to secure four causeways exiting from Utah Beach. After the division was activated as an airborne unit in 1942, its first commander, Major General William C. Lee, told them they had 'no history' but 'a rendezvous with destiny'. Although Lee led the division through its training in the United States and deployment to England, a heart attack meant he had to step down as the 101st's commander before D-Day. His replacement, Maxwell D. Taylor, was the first Allied general to land in France, and from 1962 to 1964 would serve as the Chairman of the Joint Chiefs of Staff, the highest-ranking officer in the American armed forces. The 101st lived up to Lee's expectations.

From D-Day to the end of the war, they would spend 214 days in combat, suffer 11,458 casualties, and take 29,527 enemies as prisoners of war.

48 millimetres long

BAD WEATHER AND POOR VISIBILITY meant that airborne units would often be scattered after landing and need a subtle way to identify themselves to each other without alerting the enemy. To solve this, paratroopers in the 101st were given 'crickets', a children's toy made of brass that was just less than five centimetres long. It made a 'click-clack' noise when pressed. To respond and identify yourself, the cricket needed to be pressed twice to produce a double 'click-clack' sound. The Allies also used the code word 'flash' when approaching an unknown person – the correct response, which identified one as a friendly, was 'thunder'. The third response word was 'welcome'. This was selected because Germans would have trouble pronouncing the 'w'.

14 Comanche 'code talkers'

THE US FOURTH INFANTRY DIVISION, commanded by Major General Raymond O. 'Tubby' Barton, was bound for Utah Beach, the westernmost of the landing areas. The Fourth was the only unit to use 'code talkers' during D-Day. These men were Native

Americans, frequently used in the Pacific Theatre, who transmitted instructions and messages over radio. Their communications were virtually intelligible to any non-speakers who might pick up their signal. As an added layer of secrecy, each group of code talkers would make up their own terms for words that did not exist in their language (for example, bombers became 'pregnant birds' and tanks became 'turtles'). The fourteen code talkers who landed at Utah on D-Day were Comanche speakers, part of the Fourth Signal Company. The last surviving member, Corporal Charles Chibitty, died in 2005.

5 commanders in a year

JOINING THE FOURTH on Utah Beach would be elements of the Ninetieth Infantry Division. Together they would aim to secure a beachhead. This would anchor the Allied western flank and provide a base for the attack on the nearby town of Cherbourg. The Ninetieth was founded in 1917, drawing its men from Texas and Oklahoma, and had an interlocking 'T-O' as their insignia. After being reactivated in 1942, they recruited nationwide, but retained the 'T-O', which now stood for 'Tough Ombres'. The unit suffered from unsettled leadership. The Ninetieth's commander at the start of the war, Henry Terrell, Jr., was promoted in January 1944. His replacement, Jay W. MacKelvie, an artillery specialist who had risen from the ranks to become a general, led the division on D-Day. He was deemed to be an ineffective combat leader and removed from command in July. Succeeding him was Eugene M. Landrum, who argued with his subordinates and lasted under two months. By now General Bradley regarded the Fourth as a 'problem division'. Fortunately the next commander, Raymond S. MacLain, began to improve the division's effectiveness, but was promoted in October. He was followed by James A. Van Fleet (who had coached the University of Florida's American football team in the 1920s and who President Harry S Truman would later call 'the greatest general we have ever had'), who completed the rehabilitation of the unit into a respected fighting division.

36 years old

THE MAIN GERMAN unit defending Cherbourg and the coast around Utah Beach was the 709th Static Infantry Division, which was formed in May 1941. Their commander was *Generalleutnant* Karl-Wilhelm von Schlieben, an experienced veteran of the Eastern Front. However, his men were far from being crack troops. The 709th was mainly composed of men previously seen as overage for military service. In 1944 its average age was thirty-six. They were joined by many *Ostlegionen* troops from the East, who were usually ineffective and highly unreliable in battle. Also protecting the Cotentin Peninsula was *Generalleutnant* Wilhelm Falley's Ninety-First Infantry Division. Despite only being formed that January, this was a far tougher, better-trained division than the 709th.

1 The First Division

THE FIRST INFANTRY DIVISION (also known as 'The Big Red One' or 'The Fighting First') has been in continuous, illustrious, service since 1917. During World War I they were the first American unit to arrive in France, the first to suffer casualties, the first to mount a major offensive, and the first to enter Germany. Their distinguished record continued when they were the first American division to invade North Africa and Sicily. Their commander Terry Allen stated during these campaigns that, 'nothing in hell must stop the First Division'. Despite their fighting prowess, the division was seen as ill-disciplined and rough. When Allen was promoted, Clarence R. Huebner was appointed their commanding officer in August 1943. He was charged with providing stricter leadership. Though unpopular at first, he prepared the division for their landing at Omaha Beach and exemplary record in the subsequent fighting in France and Germany. During the war 43,743 men served in the division, which suffered 21,023 casualties.

205.5 per cent battle casualty rate

UNLIKE THE FIRST, who they joined at Omaha Beach, the Twenty-Ninth Infantry Division was untried in combat. After training in Maryland they travelled to England on the Cunard ocean liner *Queen Mary* in 1942. Their commander, Charles H. Gerhardt combined authoritarianism (he was a stickler for detail and cleanliness) with a certain moral laxity (later in the war he would allow a brothel to be opened for his men near the town of Rennes). The Twenty-Ninth experienced 27,776 casualties. This was double its normal complement of 14,000. The overall aim at Omaha was to secure a five-mile-deep beachhead, and link up with the landing forces at Utah and Gold, to the west and east, respectively.

19 standing orders

THE US ARMY RANGERS' history stretches back to before the American War of Independence. In 1757, during the French and Indian War, Major Robert Rogers drew up nineteen standing orders for his Ranger company, still in place today. They included: 'Don't forget nothing', 'Don't never take a chance you don't have to', and 'Don't sit down to eat without posting sentries'. After the American Civil War, there were no Ranger units active until the name was revived in 1942. Modelled on the

British Commandos, but embodying the heritage of the 'Ranger' name, they would be the elite of the American armed forces. These volunteers were trained for endurance, cunning, and the ability to operate behind enemy lines. Eventually six Ranger battalions were formed, each made up of around 500 men. Two of them (the Second and Fifth) would participate in the landings at Omaha Beach.

50 per cent of officers without combat experience

DEFENDING THE COAST between Carentan and Bayeux was the 352nd Infantry Division, commanded by *Generalleutnant* Dietrich Kraiß. This division had been activated in November 1943 and arrived in Normandy the next month. Unlike many other German divisions it was actually at full strength (over 12,000). It was mostly made up of teenage recruits drawn from the Hanover region. Around half of the officers had no combat experience, and there was a thirty per cent shortfall in the desired number of NCOs. However, the presence of veterans of the Eastern Front from the same region of Germany negated many of these problems. They formed the nucleus of the division, and their combat experience and example meant that the 352nd would offer some of the fiercest opposition on D-Day, particularly at Omaha Beach.

5 miles long

THE CENTRAL INVASION AREA was Gold Beach, located in the five miles between the villages of Le Hamel and La Rivière. The Fiftieth (Northumbrian) Infantry Division, commanded by Major General Douglas Graham, would lead the assault. Their objective was to seize the area around the village of Arromanches, where the Allies hoped to install a Mulberry harbour, and then reach the town of Bayeux.

14,500 Canadians

ATTACKING JUNO BEACH was the task of the Third Canadian Infantry Division, supplemented by tanks and other mobile weapons from the Second Canadian Armoured Brigade. They were to support the drive towards Caen from Sword and attempt to seize the airfield at the village of Carpiquet. Around 14,500 Canadian soldiers landed at Juno on D-Day. Their commander was Major General Rod Keller. He was popular with his men for his outspoken language, although this, combined with a drinking problem and some lapses in security, made him unpopular with senior Allied officers. Keller was wounded by friendly fire on 8 August and was succeeded by Major General Daniel Spry. Keller would receive no further commands.

197 machine-gun pits

THE 716TH STATIC INFANTRY DIVISION, like the 709th, was mostly made up of conscripts in their mid-thirties. Under the command of *Generalleutnant* Wilhelm Richter, they defended a long swathe of the Normandy coast from Carentan to the Orne estuary. As such, there were elements of the 716th at every landing beach except Utah. Despite being 5,000 under their nominal strength of around 12,000, the 716th were mostly deployed in a strong defensive network of fortifications and bunkers, and had a range of weaponry including 197 machine-gun pits, seventy-five mortars, and 249 flamethrowers.

1,200 rounds per minute

AT THE START OF THE WAR the main German machine gun was the MG 34 (from *Maschinengewehr* – German for 'machine gun'), which could fire up to 900 rounds per minute. It combined lightness with accuracy and a high rate of fire. It was superseded by the even more impressive MG 42, which was issued in 1942. It was capable of firing 1,200 rounds of 7.92 millimetre cartridges per minute. From its introduction to the end of the war 414,964 of these weapons were produced. The distinctive ripping noise the MG 42 made when fired gave rise to its nickname, 'Hitler's Saw'. It was far superior to Allied machine guns like the Bren and Browning, which could fire at half the rate of the MG 42. Machine-gun squads armed with MG 42s ensconced in the bunkers of the Atlantic Wall would be one of the first, and most terrifying, barriers the Allied landing forces faced. Capable of even higher rates of fire was the MG 81, which was used as an aircraft armament by the Luftwaffe. It could fire at a rate of 1,600 rounds per minute.

25,000 commandos trained

TWO BRITISH COMMANDO (also known as 'Special Service') brigades were to be deployed on D-Day at Sword, Juno, and Gold beaches. These men, volunteers from the Army and Marines, were some of the toughest and best-trained in the Allied armed forces. Most of them had gone through an arduous training regime at the 'Commando Basic Training Centre', established in February 1942. This was located at Achnacarry Castle, a remote estate in the Scottish Highlands. Ben Nevis, Britain's highest mountain, was eighteen miles away. By the end of their training, commandos were expected to be able to run there and reach the 4,406-foot summit in a day. Nearby lochs and rivers were used for teaching amphibious landing and boat handling. In command of the school was Colonel Charles Vaughan, a somewhat portly veteran of World War I.

Vaughan demanded the highest standards of his students. As soon as recruits arrived at nearby Spean Bridge Railway Station, they had to make an eight-mile run to Achnacarry in full kit. Accommodations were spartan (either Nissen huts or canvas tents) and rations were limited. In addition to endurance and survival skills, recruits were given advanced weaponry training and instructed in unarmed and silent combat. Most training exercises took place under live fire and many were at night. Standards were high: recruits who could not complete the training were 'RTUed' (returned to their original unit). By 1945, 25,000 men (including numerous foreign nationals) had completed the six-week course at Achnacarry. Louis Mountbatten noted, 'Achnacarry could hardly have been bettered for the site, and Charles Vaughan could certainly not have been bettered as the man'.

7,473 soldiers at the Battle of Waterloo

THE THIRD INFANTRY DIVISION was one of the oldest in the British Army. It was formed in 1809 by the Duke of Wellington, and fought at Waterloo. In 1940, the division, then led by Montgomery, had been evacuated from Dunkirk. On D-Day the Third was bound for Sword, the smallest and easternmost of the landing beaches. After landing they were to attempt to capture Caen, a town of 54,000 that was the hub of the local road network. From there Paris would be only 149 miles away. The Third's commander was Major General Tom Rennie, a Scot who had been captured by the Germans during the Battle of France, but had managed to escape to freedom. Several other units supplemented the Third, including commandos from Special Service Brigades and swimming tanks from the Twenty-Seventh Armoured Brigade.

22:56

OPERATION TONGA was an ambitious plan to secure the approaches to Caen. This would allow the amphibious landing forces to break out from the beaches and also prevent the Germans reinforcing the coast. They were also charged with destroying a battery at Merville, which could bombard Sword Beach. Major General Richard Nelson Gale's Sixth Airborne Division, whose symbol was the mythical winged horse Pegasus, would carry out the operation. The first phase of the mission (Operation Deadstick) was a glider landing of 380 men tasked with capturing two strategically vital bridges crossing the Orne River and Caen Canal. They left Tarrant Rushton airfield, in Dorset, at 22:56 on 5 June, aiming to land just after midnight. Over the next few hours around 8,000 more troops from the Sixth Airborne would be landed in the area. The success of Deadstick was vital to the overall mission. If the Germans were able to destroy the bridges it would leave the bulk of the Sixth Airborne completely cut off from the rest of the Allied forces.

2,000 North African veterans

THE ONLY ARMOURED UNIT in the direct vicinity of the landing beaches was the Twenty-First Panzer Division, based near Caen. The original Twenty-First had been part of the Afrika Corps but was mostly destroyed in Tunisia in May 1943. A couple of months later the division was re-formed under the command of Edgar Feuchtinger. Two thousand members of the original division who had been recovering from wounds and sickness in Germany when it was destroyed formed the experienced core of the new Twenty-First. Initially the unit used largely obsolete French tanks, but just before D-Day it was strengthened by the arrival of 117 Panzer IV tanks. Feuchtinger left the day-to-day management of the division to his highly able deputy *Oberst* Hans von Luck, preferring to spend most of his time in Paris with his girlfriend. Later in the war Feuchtinger would be sentenced to death for misappropriation of army property and using his position to keep friends out of combat. Only a pardon from Hitler spared him. Feuchtinger was ordered back to the front, but deserted and managed to surrender to the British.

224 pounds of explosives

ONE OF THE MOST INNOVATIVE German weapons was the Goliath tank. It was a remote-controlled tracked mine, about four feet long and a foot tall, containing 224 pounds of explosives and powered by a small petrol engine. The operator manoeuvred the Goliath using a joystick and could detonate it when it was in the desired position, be it enemy fortifications, tanks, or troops. Its main vulnerability (along with its slowness and thin armour) was that over two thousand feet of cable connected the Goliath to its controller. At D-Day Allied artillery blasts would damage many of these cables, rendering most of the Goliath tanks at Normandy completely useless.

5-second fuse

THE MOST DISTINCTIVE GERMAN weapon was the Model 24 grenade, which had been in use since World War I. Easily identifiable thanks to its long handle, the 'potato masher', as British troops called it, had a six-ounce explosive charge of TNT encased in a thin metal head. This was attached to a hollow wooden handle that made it easier to throw the grenade. A distance of thirty yards was easily achievable. This was about double the distance that egg-shaped grenades could be thrown. Once armed, the stick grenade had a five-second delay fuse, and produced a blast radius of around fourteen yards.

2,000 yards

ONE OF THE MAIN WEAPONS awaiting the Allies was the eighty-eight millimetre artillery gun. It was part of the 'Flak' (from *Flugzeugabwehrkanone*, German for 'aircraft-defence cannon') series of guns but it could be used just as effectively against land targets as those in the air. Around 18,000 of these guns were produced during the war. The eighty-eight was mounted on a cross-shaped frame, which allowed it to be fired in any direction. Wheels were attached to the frame, meaning it could be towed into new positions quickly and easily. After firing, it ejected empty shells, which meant it could be reloaded simply by inserting a new shell. This meant the eighty-eight could fire up to twenty rounds a minute. It was also highly accurate. A version of this gun was mounted on the Tiger, a heavy German tank. The eighty-eight could destroy Allied tanks at a range of 2,000 yards. Having a shot from this distance would be rare during the close fighting in the battle for Normandy.

5 foot 6 inches tall

IN 1943, THE FÜHRER approved the creation of a Waffen-SS (the military wing of the SS) division, mostly composed of seventeen-year-old Hitler Youth members. They had to be at least five foot six inches tall. The 16,000 teenage volunteers were given four weeks of training. Many were so young their rations included sweets rather than tobacco and alcohol. Combined with seasoned Waffen-SS soldiers from the Eastern Front, they would form the Twelfth SS Panzer Division *Hitlerjugend* ('Hitler Youth'). The division was to be held in reserve to counter the Allied invasion and could only be deployed on Hitler's orders. The division, all determined to fight for Hitler to the death, numbered over 20,540 men, making it around twice the size of an average infantry division. They were armed with over 150 tanks and armoured guns. Their numbers included Rudolf von Ribbentrop, the son of the German foreign minister, and Hans Hermann Junge, the husband of one of Hitler's private secretaries, Traudl. The Allies would nickname them the 'Baby Division'. Fortunately for the Allies, they were too far from the landing sites to play a role in D-Day. Decoded German messages revealed that on the eve of D-Day, they would be based in the village of Évreux, which was nearer to Paris than the Normandy coast. Even further away, in Chartres, was another elite Panzer force, the *Lehr* Division - so large it had taken eighty-four trains to transport them to France from Hungary. Their name came from the German for 'teacher' (*Lehrer*), as the division showed others how to fight. That so many German forces were held in reserve, away from the Normandy beaches, would be crucial to the success of D-Day.

500 dummies

OPERATION TITANIC was a British plan to deceive the Germans about the location of the landing areas for Allied paratroopers. At 2 a.m. on 6 June, forty Royal Air Force aircraft parachuted around 500 stuffed dummies over the Normandy region – a far larger area than the actual landings were planned to be. The dummies, nicknamed 'Ruperts', were rather primitive figures made of sackcloth stuffed with straw. Each had an explosive attached, timed to go off after landing to prevent the Germans discovering the decoy immediately. Accompanying the dummies were twelve commandos from the Special Air Service. Their mission was to engage German forces, but allow some to flee so they could spread word of the landings. To swell their numbers, they carried amplifiers that played recordings of shouted orders and rifles and mortars going off. These were played for half an hour before the commandos withdrew. Two of the aircraft were lost during the operation and eight of the commandos were killed or captured. The operation did successfully divert German reserve forces away from planned drop zones, as well as the Omaha and Gold landing beaches. Deciphered German communications showed that local commanders believed the landings were genuine. The German commandant at Le Havre sent a telegram at 3.30 a.m. to Berlin stating that there had been a major landing in the area. As a result of Operation Titanic, an entire German regiment would spend the morning of D-Day searching the woods around Isigny for paratroopers who did not exist whilst Allied troops landed at nearby Omaha Beach.

Chapter 4:
The D-Day Landings

00:16

AT SIXTEEN MINUTES AFTER MIDNIGHT a Horsa glider crash-landed into the Caen Canal. It was just over fifty yards from its objective, a swing bridge. The twenty-eight men aboard, commanded by Lieutenant Den Brotheridge, were the first platoon of 'D' Company of the Oxfordshire and Buckinghamshire Light Infantry Regiment. They were the first Allied troops to arrive in France on D-Day. Five other gliders landed in the vicinity, carrying 350 more men, including their commander, Major John Howard. Their mission (Operation Deadstick) was to capture crossings over the Caen Canal and the River Orne, 400 yards away. This would prevent the Germans sending armoured reinforcements to Sword. Brotheridge led his platoon to attack the bridge, guarded by fifty men. They were spotted by an eighteen-year-old private,

Helmut Romer, who fired a flare before hiding in a mulberry bush. The crossing was captured in five minutes. Brotheridge was mortally wounded during the assault, the first Allied death of D-Day. Romer and some of his compatriots remained hidden and survived by drinking canal water. They surrendered on 7 June and spent the rest of the war in a prisoner of war camp near Calgary, Canada. At about the same time the bridge over the Orne was secured. The German counter-attack arrived at 02:00. They deployed Panzers, mortars, infantry, snipers, gunboats, and an aircraft (luckily the bomb it dropped did not detonate). The British troops managed to hold the bridges until reinforcements arrived from Sword. In their honour the bridges over the Orne and the Caen Canal were renamed Horsa and Pegasus Bridge, respectively.

7,200,000 pounds of bombs

ALLIED AIRCRAFT DROPPED over seven million pounds of bombs on D-Day. One B-17 Flying Fortress alone was capable of carrying sixteen 500-pound bombs. Their mission was to knock out batteries, reduce fortifications, and destroy obstacles. It was hoped the blast craters would create useful defensive positions. Despite many sorties being flown at lower altitudes than was usual, there were few losses. Despite the huge volume of bombs dropped, the aerial bombardment was not a resounding success in all areas. Cloud cover had meant that many of the bombs were off target, leaving many defensive positions largely intact.

113 Allied aircraft shot down

NOT ONE OF THE 10,521 combat aircraft that flew over France on D-Day was lost to action by Luftwaffe aircraft, although 113 were shot down by flak batteries. Allied airmen, including personnel from the Commonwealth and exiles from Nazi-occupied countries, as well as Britain, Canada, and the United States, flew approximately 15,000 sorties on D-Day, whereas as German aircraft were able to fly just 319.

700 feet

TO REDUCE THE TIME they spent in the air, American paratroopers were usually dropped from their C-47s at a height of no more than 700 feet (they flew at the relatively slow speed of around 120 miles per hour to make it easier to find the landing zones). This combination of low height and speed made the paratroopers' planes easier targets for German anti-aircraft fire. As they were dropping from this relatively low height, the paratroopers had to deploy their T-5 parachutes almost as soon as they jumped.

To do this, the bags the parachutes were packed into were attached to a 'static line' on the aircraft. When the paratrooper jumped out of the airplane, the line pulled tight. This ripped the cover off the bag, opening the parachute. Half of the parachutes had white canopies (rather than camouflage green), which made them stand out against the sky and an easier target.

18 Pathfinder teams

TEAMS OF 'PATHFINDERS' were created to arrive before the main force and mark drop zones as well as secure them against the enemy. Once they landed, the Pathfinders would turn on an electronic transponder called the 'Eureka'. This received and rebroadcast the electronic signal sent out by transceivers (called the 'Rebecca') on the airplanes carrying the main paratrooper force, allowing them to home in on the drop zone. The Pathfinders used signal lights to help airborne units time their jumps. On D-Day there would be eighteen teams of Pathfinders, three for each main drop zone. They landed shortly after midnight; the first American troops to arrive in France.

$10,000

ALL AMERICAN SERVICEMEN were required to take out a $10,000 life-insurance policy.

00:48

AT 00:48 MEN FROM THE 101st Airborne Division began to be dropped over the south-east of the Cotentin Peninsula. The assault, Mission Albany, aimed to secure four exits from Utah, as well as other strategic positions in the vicinity. Heavy flak and cloud cover severely disrupted the operation. Even twenty-two hours after they dropped, divisional command could only assemble 2,500 out of their 6,600 men. Despite this rocky start, the mission was largely a success and the 101st captured most of its objectives.

6 pounds

AMERICAN PARATROOPER UNITS were equipped with the SCR-536 handheld two-way radio, better known as the 'walkie-talkie'. Developed by Galvin Manufacturing (now Motorola), it weighed just six pounds and had a one-mile range. Also available was the SCR-300, a larger, more powerful, backpack-mounted radio, which had a range of five miles. Had conditions been ideal, they could have used the walkie-talkie to coordinate their forces. Many of the radios were lost or damaged in the drop, the scattering of the troops put many out of range, and the Germans were able to jam some Allied radio transmissions.

04:30

SAINTE MÈRE ÉGLISE was at the intersection of two main roads, which the Germans could use to launch counter-attacks against Utah and Omaha. It was the main target of 'Mission Boston', an aerial assault of over 6,000 men from the Eighty-Second Airborne. Most of the units landed off target. The exception was at Sainte Mère Église. The 505th Parachute Infantry Regiment landed at their appointed drop-zone at 01:40. After a firefight, the Americans captured the town. At 04:30, before dawn broke, the stars and stripes were raised over Sainte Mère Église, making it one of the first places in France to be liberated. The 505th was awarded the prestigious Presidential Unit Citation for their actions. However, the rest of the Eighty-Second was scattered and vulnerable. Three days after landing, the division was still at one-third strength and 4,000 of its men were missing. Nonetheless, they managed to regroup and were ready to fight off German counter-attacks. The Eighty-Second would remain in action for over a month before being pulled back to England. In his after-action report their commanding officer, Major General Ridgway, summed up their performance as: 'Thirty-three days of action without relief, without replacements. Every mission accomplished. No ground gained ever relinquished.'

36 men drowned

BEFORE D-DAY, ROMMEL had ordered the opening of the locks at the mouth of the Merderet River, which flooded great swathes of the countryside to a depth of over three feet. This was a great danger to the heavily laden paratroopers. Thirty-six men of the Eighty-Second would drown upon landing in these flooded areas, weighed down by their equipment.

867 gliders

GLIDERS SUPPLEMENTED the parachute landings, with 867 (a mixture of British Horsas and the smaller American Waco) being deployed. As the gliders cruised at just 1,000 feet and were mostly made of balsa wood, they were easy targets. Rough landings, sometimes under heavy fire, added to the danger. For example, 100 British glider pilots were killed or wounded on D-Day. American gliders, which began to land after 4 a.m., provided vital support for the paratroopers of the Eighty-Second and 101st. They delivered reinforcements and supplies as well as heavy equipment such as bulldozers, jeeps, and anti-tank guns.

1 in 6 paratroopers

Despite their attempts at ensuring the paratroopers would land in the planned drop zones, airborne operations on D-Day were beset with difficulties. As a result of bad weather, anti-aircraft fire, and inaccurate deployment, just one out of six Allied paratroopers reached their planned landing points. This did have an unintended positive side effect. As the paratroopers were scattered over such a wide area, it meant the Germans would vastly overestimate the size of the airborne force landing in France.

1,400 missions

C-47s flew 1,400 missions on D-Day, dropping paratroopers, equipment, and supplies over France. The next day these sturdy aircraft would fly 700 more missions to resupply the Allied armies fighting to gain a toehold in France.

150 troops

Merville Battery was believed to be a major threat to Sword. It was protected by 200 men, machine guns, barbed wire, minefields, and ditches. The task of capturing it before the amphibious landings was given to Lieutenant Colonel Terence Otway's Ninth Parachute Battalion. This was part of Operation

Tonga, the British airborne landings to secure the area behind Sword. The plan to take Merville was to land 690 men by parachute and assemble near the battery. At 04:30, sixty more men would arrive by glider and crash-land into the battery, beginning the attack. To signal that the attack would take place, the paratroopers were supposed to fire a flare. If the battery was not reduced by 05:15, British ships would begin firing on the position. The paratroopers landed after midnight, but were badly scattered. By 02:30 Otway had only assembled 150 men. Most of their equipment was missing; they had only one machine gun and no mortars, anti-tank guns, radios, or mine detectors. Also missing were the flares to signal the gliders. When the gliders arrived at 04:30 and saw no signal, the pilots assumed something had gone wrong and did not land. After he saw the gliders fly overhead, Otway launched a frontal assault. After twenty minutes the Germans surrendered. Half of Otway's force were dead or wounded. One of his officers released a carrier pigeon, which flew back to England carrying the message that Merville was captured. The four guns at Merville turned out to be outdated French seventy-five millimetre pieces. Otway dropped Gammon grenades (two-pound balls of plastic explosive) down the barrels to disable them. Overall, Operation Tonga was a major success, severely limiting the German ability to coordinate counter-attacks in the area.

2,240 SAS troops

THE BRITISH ARMY's Special Air Service (SAS) was the brainchild of Lieutenant David Stirling, an officer then serving in North Africa. He envisaged elite bands of troops who could parachute behind enemy lines, gathering intelligence, raiding, and sabotaging. Initially made up of four officers and sixty men, they went into action in 1941 and mounted a series of successful missions in North Africa and Italy. Their signature piece of equipment was a jeep with front- and rear-mounted Vickers machine guns, which gave them mobility and firepower. The SAS steadily increased in size, with Free French and Belgian troops also recruited. In 1944, the SAS was formed into a brigade of the Army Air Corps, made up of five regiments (two British, two French, and one Belgian). During D-Day, 2,240 SAS troops were dropped across the French coastline. Their mission was to mount raids to divert German attention from Normandy. Once the invasion had taken place, the SAS launched Operation Houndsworth in the Dijon region. In coordination with the French Resistance, they disrupted German attempts to send reinforcements to Normandy. The main railway line in the area was attacked twenty-two times, seventy vehicles were destroyed, and 220 casualties were inflicted.

12 noon

GERD VON RUNDSTEDT, despite being the nominal commander-in-chief in the West, was hamstrung by Germany's command structure. His position had been somewhat undermined by the arrival of Rommel in November 1943 to oversee improvements of the coastal defences. More seriously, many of the most effective military units in France could only be moved on Hitler's direct orders. On 5 June, Rommel had left France for Germany to celebrate his wife's fiftieth birthday (which would fall on D-Day) and meet with Hitler. Rommel had been told by German meteorologists that the weather conditions meant an invasion, over the next fortnight was impossible. As soon as Rommel was told of the invasion he drove back to his headquarters in France (Allied air superiority made it too dangerous to drive). His dynamic leadership would have been decisive whilst the landings were taking place. Meanwhile, Rundstedt was desperately trying to organize a German counter-offensive. After being informed of the size of the airborne landings, he was convinced that the main coastal invasion would be in Normandy. Two hours before the beach landings began, Rundstedt attempted to move his armoured reserves (the formidable Twelfth SS Panzer Division *Hitlerjugend* and the elite Panzer-*Lehr*-Division) to the Normandy coast. However, Alfred Jodl, the Chief of the Operations Staff of the *Oberkommando der*

Wehrmacht ('OKW' – the high command of all the German armed forces), ordered him not to do so. Only Hitler had the authority to move these divisions. Unfortunately for the Germans, Hitler, a habitual late riser, was asleep and not to be disturbed. He finally woke up at noon, and did not give the order to move the armoured reserves until four hours later. Had these units been deployed earlier, they could have seriously damaged the beach landings.

12,000 yards

THE GERMAN BATTERY near the village of Longues-sur-Mer was situated on a cliff between Omaha and Gold. It contained a command post and four 152-millimetre navy guns housed in concrete bunkers. The Allies had tried to destroy it with an aerial bombardment the night before D-Day. Most of the 1,500 tons of bombs dropped missed the battery and landed on the nearby village. At 05:37 Allied ships began to fire on the battery. The Germans returned fire but were unable to cause any damage. Inaccuracy beset most German batteries on D-Day. The Allied bombardment had cut off telephone communication with their observation posts, and it was too smoky for the batteries to see signal flags. In addition, there were no Luftwaffe spotter planes to report back on the accuracy of their bombardments. No Allied ships were sunk as a result of bombardment from land. At

Longues-sur-Mer, HMS *Ajax* and HMS *Argonaut* hit the battery from a range of 12,000 yards (nearly seven miles), leaving only one of the guns operational. The following day the 180 men remaining in the battery surrendered to the 231st Infantry Brigade, who had landed at Gold.

14,000 rockets launched

BEFORE THE LANDINGS took place, Allied ships unleashed a huge naval bombardment. Despite its size, it was ineffective in destroying the reinforced concrete German fortifications – although many of the troops inside were deafened or concussed. Rommel had built many concrete casemates but not put any guns in them. These 'dummy batteries' were vital in drawing away attention from operational positions. As the landing craft were closing in on the beaches, the Allies launched a huge rocket attack. To this end, Landing Craft Tanks were modified to house launching racks for the British RP-3 rocket, which had a sixty-pound warhead and a range of 1,000 yards. Each LCT(R), the 'R' stood for rocket, could carry 1,044 rockets on its upper deck and an additional 5,000 on its lower deck. They were fired in twenty-four successive bursts. In total, around 14,000 rockets were fired. They did little damage. Most of them fell into surf. Others landed on the beaches, causing grass fires and setting off mines.

1,127 rounds

SOME ALLIED SHIPS closed as near as 800 yards to the landing beaches to provide close fire support after the landings took place. Guided by spotters, they were sometimes even able to target individual German soldiers. The USS *Carmick* alone, stationed at Omaha, was able to fire 1,127 rounds of five-inch shells on D-Day. Most Allied destroyers fired between 500 and 1,000 rounds onto the landing beaches. Their accurate bombardments helped pin down the Germans and allowed the land forces to make headway.

400 cubic centimetres

NO ONE WAS UNDER any illusions that the struggle to secure the beaches at Normandy would result in casualties. The soldiers of the Allied invasion forces were given tin cans containing two 400 cubic centimetre bottles. One contained distilled water, the other dried plasma. Plasma is the part of blood that holds the blood cells. It is prepared by spinning fresh blood in a centrifuge, which splits off the plasma component. When needed, the plasma and water were combined and ready for transfusion in three minutes. Responsible for safely producing huge quantities of plasma for the American armed forces was an African-American surgeon called Charles R. Drew. Drew was unable to reverse the absurd American policy of racially segregating blood donations. However, under Drew's leadership, by 1945 the Red Cross Blood Bank in New York City had collected enough blood to produce six million packages of plasma.

100,000,000 units

THE AMERICAN PHARMACEUTICAL industry was able to produce one hundred million units of penicillin in May 1944, the month before Operation Overlord took place.

21 per cent

PROVIDING EFFECTIVE MEDICAL CARE on D-Day was a major problem. The amphibious assault force would face its largest numbers of wounds and injuries before sufficient numbers of medical troops and equipment could be put ashore to care for them. In the early hours of the invasion it would be impossible to treat them in France. Medical battalions went ashore with the first waves of troops to collect the wounded and set up emergency surgical centres. The injured who could be moved would be loaded on DUKWs and LCVPs on the beaches. They would be taken to one of 153 LSTHs (which stood for 'Landing Ship, Tanks (Hospitals)' – LSTs that were converted for medical use), which would take them back to hospitals in England. Each one could hold up to 300 men on stretchers on the tank deck, as well as crowd 300 more walking wounded on the upper decks and crew quarters. There was a team of medical personnel on each LSTH to care for the men. Thanks to these plans, twenty-one per cent of Allied wounded on D-Day were operated on in the first hour, and another forty-seven per cent in the next six hours.

28,000 No. 24 smoke generators

SMOKE SCREENS were used to conceal Allied movements from the Germans. The main piece of equipment used were British No. 24 smoke generators. This utilized zinc chloride to produce a dense white smoke. Each generator weighed about forty pounds and could emit clouds of smoke for between twelve and fifteen minutes. The British Pioneer Corps (who were trained to carry out light engineering under combat conditions) manned the generators – which put out over 140,000 gallons of smoke. Twenty-three Pioneer companies (6,700 men) went ashore on D-Day, conducting a range of tasks from stretcher-bearing to clearing obstacles, to laying ramps on the beach for Allied vehicles. Twenty-five days after D-Day over 25,000 Pioneers had landed in Normandy.

36-man capacity

Eisenhower believed the Landing Craft, Vehicle, Personnel (or LCVP) was crucial to the success of the D-Day landings. Its creator was Andrew Higgins, who had designed shallow-draft boats for oil companies exploring the swamps of southern Louisiana. Higgins had won the contract to build landing craft despite his abrasive personality (he had stated the American Navy 'doesn't know one damn thing about small boats'). His assembly lines in New Orleans employed 30,000 people to construct LCVPs, producing 20,000 of them during the war. They were paid top dollar regardless of race or gender. The LCVP was thirty-six-feet long and ten-and-a-half-feet wide, and could carry thirty-six men (or a jeep and twelve men). It was mostly made of plywood but had a metal ramp at the front, and two machine guns at the rear. On D-Day LCVPs were carried on LSTs and lowered into the water, ready for troops to come aboard. The shallow draft of the LCVP meant it would bob and shake heavily in the rough waters of the Channel. However, it could move right up to the beach, lower the ramp, quickly unload, and return to its mother ship to take on more men. More Americans went ashore in LCVPs than in all other types of craft combined.

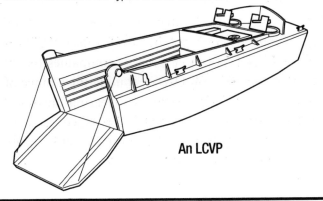

An LCVP

8 Goliaths

THE STRONGEST GERMAN position at Utah was a blockhouse at La Madeleine, which had three cannons, a howitzer, five grenade-launching mortars, two flamethrowers, three heavy machine guns, and eight Goliath tanks. Its commander was the twenty-three-year-old *Leutnant* Arthur Jahnke, who had been wounded in the East and won the Iron Cross. Rommel had visited La Madeleine on 11 May, and criticized him for not putting enough obstacles, mines, and barbed wire around the blockhouse. Rommel relented when Jahnke told him he had put up all the barbed wire he had been sent. He took off his suede officer's gloves to show him the deep scars on his hands from personally laying down the barbed wire. Before the landings took place, a wave of B-26 Marauders launched a devastating raid on La Madeleine, knocking out their communications and leaving them with just two machine guns and two grenade launchers.

56 years old

THE LANDINGS AT UTAH were scheduled to begin at 06:30 with a wave of thirty-two swimming tanks; over the next twenty-two minutes three waves of infantry and combat engineers would follow. Little went to plan. Few craft arrived on schedule and many came ashore in the wrong position, with some landing over a mile off course. In the first boats to hit the shore was Brigadier General Theodore Roosevelt III (the eldest son of former President Teddy Roosevelt), the assistant commander of the Fourth Infantry Division. Roosevelt, despite having arthritis (requiring him to use a cane) and a heart condition, was determined to go ashore. He believed the presence of a general on the beach would reassure the men. It took repeated verbal requests and a written petition to his commanding officer (Major General Barton) for him to win permission. Roosevelt was the oldest man to go ashore on D-Day. His youngest son, Captain Quentin Roosevelt II, was in the first wave at Omaha. Roosevelt's presence at Utah proved to be crucial. Realizing that many units were in the wrong position, he simply stated, 'We'll start the war from here!' Wearing a wool-knit cap (he did not like helmets), he calmly re-coordinated the landing forces, giving them new objectives and modifying the plan of attack. Roosevelt's leadership turned a potentially disastrous situation into a resounding success, and pushed inland four miles. Sadly on 12 July Roosevelt died of a heart attack in Normandy. For his actions he was posthumously awarded the Medal of Honor, the United States' highest military decoration.

110 guns

ON UTAH THE GERMANS had 110 artillery pieces, ranging in calibre from seventy-five to 170 millimetres. Further inland there were eighteen batteries – the largest one had four 210-millimetre guns.

7 days

ALFRED JODL THOUGHT it would take the Allies one week to put three divisions into France. In the wider vicinity of Utah alone (if airborne troops are included), the Americans were able to deploy three divisions in just one day. At Utah the Americans put ashore 20,000 soldiers and 1,700 motorized vehicles. Their casualties were not heavy – 187 killed or wounded.

4 per cent effective strength

LANDINGS AT OMAHA were scheduled to begin at 06:30, 'H-Hour', with swimming tanks supporting infantry. Rough seas, strong winds, and heavy currents quickly scuppered these plans. Only two tanks made it ashore. The landing craft were similarly impacted by the conditions. Only one of the nine infantry companies actually landed in its planned disembarkation point – Company 'A' of the 116th Infantry Regiment. Once they were ashore the Americans faced a formidable German defence, which occupied the cliffs that overlooked the beach. They had twelve *Widerstandnester* ('strong points') that fired across the length of the beach, cutting down the troops desperately looking for cover who were simultaneously struggling to clear the obstacles on the beach without armoured support. Casualties in the first wave were high. For example, within an hour Company 'A' had lost ninety-six per cent of its effective strength.

27 swimming tanks lost at sea

SWIMMING TANKS were supposed to play a major role in supporting the landing troops on D-Day. However, in many cases they were unable to swim ashore or had to be landed conventionally. At Omaha twenty-seven of the twenty-nine DD tanks put to sea sank before reaching land, due to a navigational error that placed them in rough water too far from the shore. Three of the tanks were unable to be launched because the ramp on their landing craft jammed. At other beaches like Sword, where waters were calmer, the DD tanks were more effective in reaching the shore and supporting infantry. In addition, ten bulldozers, supposed to clear obstacles, were lost during the landings at Omaha, and three were disabled on the beach by German fire. This left just three bulldozers operational.

5-gallon drum

MOST OF THE AMERICAN PLATOONS included two men with flamethrowers (the Commonwealth forces mainly used the Churchill Crocodile, a tank-mounted flamethrower, instead of having men carry the weapon). The men were laden with one hundred pounds of equipment, including a rifle and hand grenades, as well as a back-mounted five-gallon drum of fuel and a nitrogen cylinder to propel the flame. The weapon could launch a jet of flame over twenty yards, and was highly effective at clearing bunkers.

16 teams

AT OMAHA THERE WERE sixteen teams of five engineers, who were scheduled to land just after the first wave. They were either 'Seabees' (members of the Navy Construction Battalion) or army engineers. Their task was to blow 150-foot gaps in the beach obstacles to clear the way for infantry and armour. Heavy enemy fire and loss of equipment made their task difficult, although they were able to clear six gaps. Despite their efforts there was considerable congestion at Omaha, leading to a backlog of fifty craft circling off coast waiting to land. Compounding this, twelve of the sixteen 'beachmaster' teams who were assigned to put up flags on the beach to guide in ships never made it to shore. The four teams who did landed in the wrong place. When the second wave arrived at 07:00 they faced a chaotic situation with many companies scattered and leaderless. By 08:30 most of the beach was still bunched up with men unable to advance. However, the men rallied and managed to begin to reduce the German defences and establish a beachhead.

100-foot cliff

POINTE DU HOC WAS A one-hundred-foot-high cliff jutting out into the sea, overlooking both Omaha and Utah. It was a key German position, housing a network of trenches and six cement casemates. They housed artillery pieces, but these had been removed after the position had been bombed in April. Thus on D-Day, there were actually no heavy guns at Pointe du Hoc. The assault was given to the second and fifth battalions of the Rangers, commanded by Lieutenant Colonel James Earl Rudder. Omar Bradley called his task the most difficult command he had ever ordered. The Rangers were to land at Omaha, scale the cliff under enemy fire, and capture the position. Their secondary objective was to move inland to establish a roadblock. To scale the cliff, the Rangers used extension ladders supplied by the London Fire Department as well as grapnels attached to ropes that were fired by rocket guns. The Rangers reached the base of Pointe du Hoc at 07:10, forty minutes later than scheduled. Rough seas had scattered their landing craft (capsizing one), meaning they were at half-strength. German troops rained down gunfire and grenades from above as soon as the Rangers landed. Naval bombardment on Pointe du Hoc temporarily scattered the defenders, enabling the Rangers to begin scaling the cliff face. By 07:30 the Rangers had fought their way to the top and set about capturing the position. At 08:15 the Rangers established their roadblock near Pointe du Hoc. Over the course of the day the Germans launched five counter-attacks, but the Rangers held firm.

80 per cent

EIGHTY PER CENT of the radios sent ashore at Omaha were lost or damaged during the landing. Communications became so difficult that General Bradley briefly considered withdrawing men from Omaha to the British sector of Normandy.

320th Barrage Balloon Battalion

DURING WORLD WAR II the US Army was segregated, with black soldiers serving in separate units. Black soldiers had separate facilities – from canteens to churches. For the most part they served as auxiliaries, working as cooks, truck drivers, or unloading supplies. It was believed that black people were not suited to serve in combat. Despite this prejudice, in the Army Air Forces there was an African-American fighter group called the Tuskegee Airmen who distinguished themselves in Italy. The first black unit to come ashore on D-Day was the 320th Barrage Balloon Battalion, who landed at Omaha and Utah. Their task was to deploy VLA (very low altitude) barrage balloons, which prevented German aircraft bombing or strafing the beach. The men had striped down the 350-pound standard winch that held the tethering cables to around fifty pounds so it could be carried by one man. Working in teams of two to four (so they could cover more ground), the men of the 320th quickly went about their tasks. The balloons were floated at irregular intervals and heights (up to an altitude of 2,000 feet). Later on D-Day 1,200 black soldiers (truck drivers, port workers, and members of the Quartermaster Corps) landed at Utah. Additionally thousands of black servicemen served on the ships and landing craft in the Channel.

2,400 casualties

THE AMERICANS AT OMAHA suffered 2,400 dead, wounded, or missing on D-Day in the process of landing 34,000 men. This casualty rate was still around five per cent less than Allied war planners expected.

2,500 obstacles

THERE WERE 2,500 OBSTACLES scattered across the ten-mile width of Gold (in addition to the five miles of the landing zone that were too rocky for troops to land on). These obstacles, made of steel, concrete, or wood, weighed about 900 tons. The British began landing infantry after 07:25 and were able to unload armoured vehicles directly onto the beach. Hobart's Funnies showed their worth by neutralizing many of the obstacles. The Germans had no armour at Gold and the shore bombardment there had been highly effective. By mid-afternoon the British had been able to secure the beach and begin to drive into the French interior and link up with the Canadians from Juno.

£32,000

THE ONLY VICTORIA CROSS awarded on D-Day fetched £32,000 when it was auctioned in 1983. The Victoria Cross is the Commonwealth's highest military award for bravery in the face of the enemy. The recipient was Company Sergeant Major Stanley Hollis, a member of the 'Green Howards', an infantry regiment from Yorkshire assigned to the Fiftieth Infantry Division on D-Day. A native of Middlesbrough, Hollis had served in the army since the outbreak of the war. Hollis' company was involved in the assault at

Gold. After the landing, Hollis and his company commander discovered two German pillboxes had been bypassed. Knowing the threat they posed, Hollis rushed forward under machine-gun fire. He threw a grenade into the pillbox and fired his Sten sub-machine gun into the interior. Hollis then captured the second pillbox. The same day Hollis was part of an attack on a German artillery position. Hollis was positioned in a house that received a direct hit. He led his men to cover but realized two had been left behind in the disintegrating house. Hollis ran back into the open and under heavy fire, distracted the enemy long enough to allow the two men to escape to safety. Hollis was wounded in September and returned to England, where King George VI awarded him the Victoria Cross on 10 October. The citation read that largely thanks to Hollis 'the Company's objectives were gained ... and by his bravery he saved the lives of many of his men'. After the War Hollis worked as a landlord before his death in 1972.

24,970 troops

THE BRITISH LANDED 24,970 troops at Gold on D-Day, at a cost of 400 casualties.

4 *Widerstandnester*

THERE WERE FOUR *Widerstandnester* at one-kilometre intervals on Juno at Vaux, Courseulles, Bernières, and St-Aubin. These positions housed artillery pieces sighted to provide interlocking enfilade fire along the entire length of the beach. All of the strong points were made of concrete and surrounded by anti-tank ditches, minefields, trenches, barbed wire, and machine-gun nests. None of the positions at Juno were seriously damaged by the aerial or naval bombardment. They were manned by a mixture of teens, overage conscripts, and *Ostlegionen*. These men lacked any mobility. Troops had to walk between the strong points and large guns could only be moved by horsepower.

8 German defenders

FIVE MILES FROM the Normandy coast lies Creully. This village was a planned meeting point of British and Canadian forces advancing from Gold and Juno. The German troops stationed there had left to reinforce nearby Caen. They left behind eight defenders from the *Ostlegionen* – five Russians and three Lithuanians. After fighting their way off the beach the Sherman tanks of the First Hussars Canadian Armoured Regiment made their way inland. At around 2.30 p.m. one of their tanks, commanded by Lieutenant Bill McCormick, arrived at Creully. They quickly subdued the remaining German defenders. There was no sign of the British troops they were meant to meet up with. The First Hussars made their way forward to their primary objective for the day, the Caen–Bayeux highway. They were the only Allied landing unit to do so. For McCormick, a twenty-four-year-old, the war ended five days later. His regiment was engaged in a brutal battle at Le Mesnil-Patry. He was seriously injured and his right leg had to be amputated below the knee. Fortunately he survived, went home to Canada, and was able to return to Creully in 2011, when a square in the village was named after him,

1,200 casualties

THE CANADIANS suffered 1,200 casualties on D-Day whilst putting 21,400 men ashore.. They also landed 900 armoured vehicles, 240 field guns, 280 anti-tank guns, and 4,000 tons of supplies. Despite the difficulties they faced, the soldiers at Juno made the biggest advances – over six miles inland in some places.

64 hours

TWO BRITISH MIDGET SUBMARINES, known as X-boats, were employed to guide the landing of the troops at Sword and Juno. They acted as navigation beacons by flashing green lights for the landing craft. Each had a crew of five men who had to operate in extremely cramped conditions whilst ensuring the Germans did not spot them. As a result of the postponement of D-Day, by the time the landings took place, they had been in position for around sixty-four hours. However, they remained alert, and unspotted, and when the time came, they were able to ensure the landing craft followed the correct course and reached the beaches safely.

07:25

BRITISH TROOPS FROM the Third Division began landing on Sword Beach at 07:25. Their objective for the day was to win control of the high ground above Caen, and, if possible, the city itself, along with an airfield at nearby Carpiquet. Compared with other landing beaches, Sword was only lightly defended, with obstacles and some emplacements in sand dunes. The British were able to lay down suppressing fire and allow most of their tanks to land safely. At about the same time, three German E-boats attacked the Allied ships supporting the land troops. They launched torpedoes and sank the Norwegian destroyer *Svenner*, one of the few German naval successes on D-Day. Though the ship sank, its crew was rescued. The beach was secured and at 8.30 a.m., the leading British battalions began to push inland while more troops and artillery successfully landed. Congestion amongst the Allies and German resistance from their inland positions limited the push towards Caen. At around 4 p.m. the Twenty-First Panzer Division and the 192nd Panzer Grenadier Regiment launched a counter-attack. Ninety-eight German tanks supported by infantry pushed back the British troops from Sword. Some of the infantry managed to fight their way right back to the beach by 8 p.m., but the tanks were unable to advance to support them. The British soldiers, with the support of their own tanks and air strikes, were able to halt the German onslaught. The only significant counter-attack launched on D-Day had been defeated.

1 piper

JOINING THE THIRD DIVISION at Sword was the First Special Service Brigade, made up of British and French commandos. They landed at the east of the beach near the port of Ouistreham. In command was Brigadier Simon Fraser, Lord Lovat (and Chief of Clan Fraser). He was joined by his personal piper, Bill Millin. In defiance of official regulations that bagpipes should only be used in rear areas, Fraser ordered Millin to play his pipes as they went ashore. Millin, who was also the only man to wear a kilt during the Normandy landings, was apparently not targeted by German snipers because they thought he was insane. After this dramatic entrance, the commandos took out several German positions. They then moved inland to link up with the airborne forces at Pegasus Bridge who had landed earlier in the day.

28,845 troops

AT SWORD BEACH 28,845 TROOPS were landed by nightfall, with just 630 casualties suffered. They were unable to capture Caen, their objective of the day – it remained under German control until 6 August, but they could still be satisfied with their performance.

40 C-47s

LATE ON D-DAY, forty C-47s (known as 'Dakotas' in the Royal Air Force) from 233 Squadron took off from England to resupply the Sixth Airborne by dropping 116 tons of supplies. As they flew towards the French coast at sunset, Allied ships mistook them for enemy aircraft and fired on them. Two of the Dakotas were forced to turn back, one ditched, five went missing, and the rest scattered. The Sixth could only recover around twenty per cent of the airdrop.

15 degrees Celsius

WEATHER CONDITIONS ON 6 JUNE had not been ideal (there was a breeze and the skies were cloudy) and strong currents had pushed many of the landing craft off course. However, they were just about good enough not to seriously threaten the landings. By the end of the day, skies were partly sunny and the temperature was fifteen degrees Celsius.

156,000 troops landed

BY THE END OF D-DAY the Allies landed 156,000 soldiers in France. They suffered 10,000 casualties.

Chapter 5:
The Battle for Normandy

2,000 civilians killed

CAEN WAS A VITAL TARGET. The city was located at the centre of the local road network and astride two major waterways (the Caen Canal and the Orne River). Capturing Caen would provide a superb starting point for further advances into France. It was the target of a two-day Allied bombing campaign starting on D-Day. They had tried to safeguard the civilian populace by dropping leaflets warning them of the bombings. Only a few hundred were able to leave. During the bombings one-quarter of the city's population sheltered in the tunnels below Caen, part of medieval stone quarries. There were 2,000 civilian deaths as a result of the air raids, which reduced the city to ruins. The rubble created ideal defensive positions for the Germans, making it harder to capture the city. Caen had been the main objective for the British at

Sword. Although they had broken out from their landing zone and linked up with Canadian forces from Juno on 7 June, the Germans blocked their advance to Caen.

20 prisoners executed

THE TWELFTH SS PANZER Division had advanced into Normandy on the afternoon of D-Day. One of the regiments in the division, the Twenty-Fifth Panzer Grenadiers, had set up their command post in the Ardenne Abbey. This complex of medieval buildings was located in the village of Saint-Germain-la-Blanche-Herbe, near Caen. The regiment's commander, SS-*Standartenführer* Kurt Meyer, had a history of brutality. In Poland he had shot fifty Jews and in Ukraine he had ordered the burning and massacre of a village. On 7 June, the Germans engaged Canadian forces from Juno in the village of Authie. Captured soldiers from the North Nova Scotia Highlanders and the Twenty-Seventh Canadian Armoured Regiment were taken to the abbey. Eleven were randomly selected and executed. The next day seven more prisoners were shot in the head. On 17 June, two prisoners from the Stormont, Dundas and Glengarry Highlanders were captured whilst on patrol and executed. These executions of unarmed prisoners of war were a violation of the Geneva Convention. In 1945

Meyer was tried for his role in the atrocity. It was found that he had not executed any men himself or directly ordered the killings. However, as he had ordered his men to take no prisoners, he was found guilty of inciting the executions. He was given the death sentence, commuted to life imprisonment. Meyer was granted early release in 1954, dying of a heart attack seven years later. It is likely that 187 Canadians were executed during the first days of the Battle for Normandy, almost all by the Twelfth SS. Illegal executions were not just carried out by the Germans. There were reports of Allied soldiers killing unarmed captives.

10,000 prints processed

IN THE EARLY HOURS OF 7 JUNE, the Tenth Photographic Group (Reconnaissance) of the United States Army Air Force was in the midst of processing 10,000 images taken above Normandy. They were mostly taken to check on the accuracy of the naval bombardment.

23 times

AFTER FIGHTING OFF German resistance at Gold, the British XXX Corps was heavily involved in Operation Perch, an attempt to capture Caen. A pincer attack was launched to encircle the city. XXX

Corps was to form the western arm. They made steady progress until 9 June, when they reached Tilly-sur-Seulles, twelve miles west of Caen. This village was the focus of a German counter-attack and a bitter struggle ensued. Over the next eight days it would change hands twenty-three times before it was decisively liberated. On 13 June, the British attempted to outflank the Germans at the nearby town of Villers-Bocage, but were forced to withdraw. Meanwhile, the attack on Caen from the east had stalled. On 14 June, Montgomery called off Operation Perch.

3,132 aircraft

OMAHA HAD SEEN THE MOST concerted German resistance. However, as night fell on D-Day Plus One they showed little sign of being able to organize a counter-attack. By 8 June, most of the units that had landed at Omaha had achieved their invasion-day objectives. Although they faced harassing fire from snipers and artillery, the Americans cleared the beach of obstacles and established exit routes for traffic from the beach. Air support had been crucial. On 8 June alone, 3,132 aircraft attacked German positions around Omaha.

12,000 yards

AFTER TWO DAYS THE AMERICANS at Utah had carved out a beachhead 12,000 yards deep. Not everything had gone to plan. Due to congestion at the beach, loading at Utah was behind schedule. Many of the airborne troops in the area remained isolated. The Germans still held strong positions to the east of the Merderet River, poised to attack them.

130 'X Troopers'

THE NUMBER TEN (Inter-Allied) Commando was formed in 1942. It was made up of foreign volunteers (aside from a British headquarters' staff). A unit of foreign commandos was the idea of Lieutenant Philippe Kieffer, a Free French Naval officer serving in England. He would lead a commando troop ashore at Sword on D-Day. These foreigners received the same training as British commandos. Their local knowledge and language skills made them invaluable in the field. There were French, Dutch, Belgian, Norwegian, Polish, and Italian-speaking sections. The 'X Troop' (or 'Miscellaneous Troop') of the Inter-Allied consisted of enemy aliens, many of whom were Jewish refugees from German territories. To prevent them suffering severe retribution if captured, they all had false names and personal histories (including identification listing their religion as Church of England). One hundred and thirty men served in X Troop. In addition to combat duties, they served an important role in interrogating German prisoners.

80 one-second bursts

THE BRITISH PRODUCED 800 Churchill Crocodile tanks. Instead of a machine gun (they retained the standard seventy-five-millimetre tank gun) they had a flamethrower. It carried 400 gallons of fuel in an armoured trailer, which was enough for eighty one-second bursts at a range of 120 yards. The Crocodile was particularly effective when used against German bunkers.

3.9 inches of armour

THE GERMAN TIGER I TANK WAS THE largest tank in operation during the Battle for Normandy. It weighed fifty-seven tons, had 3.9 inches of armour, and was large enough to mount the eighty-eight-millimetre gun (designed as an anti-aircraft weapon) and two machine guns. The first Tigers rolled off the production line in August 1942. Their complexity and cost meant that just 1,347 were built until production stopped in August 1944. The Tiger was often too heavy for some bridges. It was prone to breakdowns and its high petrol consumption was problematic (it consumed over thirty tons of fuel every one hundred miles) as Germany's fuel reserves grew depleted. The Tiger outgunned Allied tanks in Normandy. At the Battle of Villers-Bocage a single Tiger destroyed fourteen tanks, fifteen personnel carriers, and two anti-tank guns in just fifteen minutes. The Germans were never able to send enough Tigers to Normandy to regularly bring this advantage to bear. In summer 1944, they introduced the even larger Tiger II (or Royal Tiger), which weighed sixty-eight tons. These were never produced in large numbers. By winter 1944, just one hundred were available for service on the Western Front.

2,500,000 men unloaded

THE ALLIES DEVELOPED portable temporary harbours, called 'Mulberries', whose components could be transported across the Channel. They would be put together in Normandy to create two square miles of harbour. This would mean supplies could be unloaded without having to capture heavily defended ports like Caen or Cherbourg. Two Mulberries were to be built: 'A' at Saint-Laurent-sur-Mer, on Omaha, and 'B' at Arromanches, on Gold. Construction began on 9 June. Ships (called 'Corn Cobs') were deliberately sunk off the Normandy coast to create an area protected from the force of the waves (called a breakwater). These areas were called 'Gooseberries'. Then huge concrete caissons (code-named Phoenixes) five stories high and displacing 6,000 tons were sunk to further calm the waters. The next stage was to deploy fifteen floating pier heads (called the 'Spud Pier'), creating four square miles of space to unload cargo. These landing wharves were connected to land by six miles of floating bridge piers (code-named the 'Whale'). The Mulberries cost £40,000,000 to build and transport. On 19 June, a three-day storm struck Normandy. Mulberry 'A', not yet fully secured, was wrecked (in addition, 600 vessels were lost). The damage was so severe that it was decided to abandon construction there. The Mulberry at Arromanches was completed and became known as Port Winston. Despite being designed to last for three months, Port Winston saw ten months of use. During this time 2,500,000 men, 500,000 vehicles, and 4,000,000 tons of supplies were unloaded there.

2,830 calories a day

AMERICANS LANDING ON D-DAY carried three K Ration boxes. Each pack provided at least 2,830 calories per day, but this was often not enough for men on combat duty. Named after its developer, Doctor Ancel Keys, each K Ration was composed of three packages of non-perishable, ready-to-eat, food enclosed in one watertight box. These could be carried in the large pockets of the American battledress. The breakfast unit contained one can of ham, veal, or eggs, a fruit paste bar, one packet of instant coffee, and water purification tablets. The dinner unit included a can of cooked ham, cheese, or ham and cheese, biscuits, caramels, salt, matches, and orange and grape powdered juice. The supper unit was composed of a can of chicken pot pie, pork with carrots, chocolate, soup powder, and toilet paper. All units also included biscuits or cookies, sugar, chewing gum, and packs containing four cigarettes. Chlorine-based Halazone water-purification tablets were included. Two were enough to purify around two pints of water, but it had to be left for half an hour before it was safe to drink. The landing troops were supposed to carry four pints of drinking water with them when they came ashore. Commonwealth soldiers carried enough food for thirty-six hours when they landed, although their ration packs were different, usually including bully beef, oatmeal, and tea.

446 tons of potatoes

ONE OF THE ALLIES' KEY considerations was stockpiling enough food to feed the troops in Normandy. Up to D-Day Plus Four (10 June) 446 tons of potatoes, ninety-eight tons of meat, sixty-one tons of bread, and fifty-one tons of vegetables were sent to the beachheads. The food stores were built up at naval victualling yards in Portsmouth and Plymouth. There were 4,500 trained army chefs amongst the invading army, a major part of the 54,000 support personnel who served in the forces that invaded Normandy.

900 people fed per week

THE ALLIES FITTED OUT TEN VESSELS as Landing Barge, Kitchens (LBKs) to support the invasion. These floating kitchens could carry enough food and water to feed 900 people for a week. In one day an LBK could turn out 1,600 hot meals and 800 cold meals, and make 1,000 pounds of bread. Each LBK had a crew of thirteen cooks, nine seamen, and three stokers.

642 civilians massacred

AFTER THE ALLIED LANDINGS, German units in France began moving towards Normandy. The French Resistance escalated its raiding and sabotage. The German treatment of the French populace became increasingly violent. By 1944, many of the German officers in France had served in the East, where brutality in response to partisan activity was the norm. On 8 June, Rundstedt gave orders to defeat the Resistance with 'swift and ruthless initiative ... carried out with the greatest severity and without leniency'. One of the units being moved was the Second SS Panzer Division *Das Reich*, making its way to Normandy from southern France. Whilst in the Limousin region of west-central France resistance guerrillas attacked the division. They retaliated by entering the village of Tulle and hanging ninety-nine of its male inhabitants on 9 June. The next day SS-*Sturmbannführer* Adolf Diekmann led his battalion to the village of Oradour-sur-Glane. They rounded up all the locals in the market square. The men were secured in barns on the outskirts of the village; women and children were locked in the church. The soldiers shot the men and set the barns and corpses on fire. They then threw explosives into the church, setting it alight. Anyone who tried to escape was gunned down. Six hundred and forty-two people were murdered. Just six men and one woman managed to escape. After the massacre Oradour-sur-Glane was looted and torched. After the war the President of France, Charles de Gaulle, ordered that the ruins be left in place as a permanent memorial.

138,000 deported

THE NAZIS DEPORTED any potential opponents to their regime in France to concentration camps. Anyone suspected of involvement with the Resistance was targeted. Up to the Liberation, 61,000 people in France were deported. Only forty per cent returned alive. The Nazis targeted France's Jewish population, which numbered around 350,000 in 1940. Persecution of Jews was rife in both occupied and Vichy France. Pétain's regime was openly anti-semitic, excluding Jews from public life, appropriating their property, and interning thousands in their detention camps. In 1942, Jews in France began to be brutally rounded up and deported to concentration camps to the east. Many French police and administrators collaborated in this process. A total of 77,000 Jews (one-third from Vichy France) were deported from France. Very few returned.

37 tanks destroyed

AT 2.30 P.M. ON 11 JUNE, Canadian forces attacked the hamlet of Le Mesnil-Patry as part of the effort to capture Caen. They had been given no information about German positions, and had had no time to send out patrols. The troops involved (infantry from the Queen's Own Rifles of Canada and Sherman tanks from the First Hussars) had no idea that the Twelfth SS Panzer Division were positioned in the hamlet. In clear daylight the Canadian tanks advanced with infantry riding them. They were easy targets for German tanks, mortars, and artillery, firing on them from just 800 yards. It soon became clear why soldiers had given the

Sherman the macabre nickname 'Ronson' (after the cigarette lighter that claimed to 'light up the first time, every time'). Numerous tanks burst into flame after being hit. The Canadians were forced to withdraw. Fifty-five of the infantry died in the battle, which an English newspaper compared to the similarly doomed Charge of the Light Brigade of the Crimean War. Le Mesnil-Patry was the bloodiest day of battle in the history of the First Hussars; they had thirty-seven tanks destroyed and fifty-nine fatalities.

326,547 troops landed

BY THE END OF D-DAY PLUS FIVE (11 June) the Allies had landed 326,547 troops in Normandy, along with 54,186 vehicles and 104,428 tons of supplies.

16,500 paratroopers dropped in one day

OPERATION MARKET-GARDEN was Montgomery's bid to bring a swift end to the war by forcing a way into Germany. The first part, 'Market', was to drop airborne forces (consisting of the American Eighty-Second and 101st Airborne Divisions, who had served so heroically in Normandy, the British First Airborne Division, and the Polish First Independent Parachute Brigade) into the Netherlands over a three-day period. They would secure eight water crossings in the Lower Rhine. In the second phase,

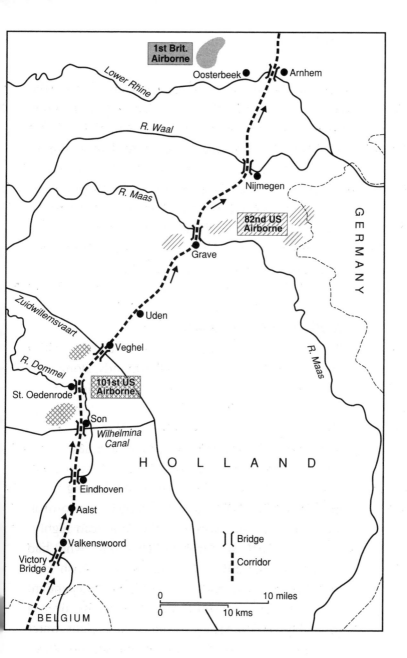

The Plan of Attack for Operation Market-Garden, 1944

'Garden', the British XXX Corps would arrive from the south. The Allies would then be able to go around the northern end of the Siegfried Line and advance into Germany. As an added benefit, they would also be in a position to destroy V-1 and V-2 launch sites in the Low Countries. Many American generals were sceptical, wanting to drive towards the Rhine through France. However, on 10 September, Eisenhower approved the plan. Its success rested on the assumption that the Germans would be unable to mount any coherent resistance. This was flawed. The Germans had recently reinforced the area. Thanks to intercepted communications, aerial photographs, and reports from the Dutch Resistance, Montgomery was warned of this, but he refused to change the plan. The operation began on 17 September with a daylight airborne invasion. That day 16,500 paratroopers and 3,500 glider-borne troops landed. After a promising start, the Allies ran into trouble. Persistent fog meant they were unable to drop as many supplies and reinforcements as scheduled. Some of the airborne forces managed to cross the Rhine into Germany, but they had no support. The Germans slowed the advance of the XXX Corps, preventing them reinforcing the airborne forces. They were left isolated and outnumbered, facing crippling shortages of food and ammunition. On 25 September, Montgomery ordered the evacuation of Allied troops from the area. Market-Garden had ended in failure.

132 men left standing

CARENTAN WAS A VITAL stepping-stone in the American drive towards Cherbourg. The Germans had flooded the area around the town, leaving only a few routes above water. On 10 June, the 101st Airborne began the attack on Carentan. The Third Battalion of the 502nd Parachute Infantry Regiment would make the first approach along the N13 highway. As they were advancing completely in the open, the Germans were able to cut the battalion to pieces. The battalion commander, Lieutenant Colonel Robert G. Cole, rallied his men under heavy fire. Nightfall appeared to offer respite – until two Stuka dive-bombers strafed the road. The Americans soon dubbed the N13 'Purple Heart Lane' (after the medal awarded to American military killed or wounded in battle). The next day Cole again displayed his courage. German troops around a farmhouse had pinned down the battalion in a ditch. Cole, after blowing a whistle, led his men over the top in a bayonet charge through an open field. After a close-quarters battle the Germans were vanquished. Just 132 of the 700 men Cole commanded were alive and uninjured. This success was vital in opening the approach to Carentan for the 101st, which was captured the next day. The German counter-attacked Carentan on 13 June in an engagement known as the Battle of Bloody Gulch. The 101st, reinforced with tanks, held firm.

Carentan was secured. Cole was awarded the Medal of Honour. He did not live to receive it – a sniper killed him during Operation Market-Garden.

4,261 flying bombs brought down

LED BY WERNHER VON BRAUN, the German research centre at Peenemünde was at the cutting edge of rocket technology. As revenge for the Allied bombings of German cities, the Nazis launched their own bombing campaign, using the *Vergeltungswaffen* ('reprisal weapons') developed there. The first was the V-1. It was essentially a guided flying bomb powered by a jet engine. The engine produced a buzzing sound, so the British nicknamed it the 'doodlebug'. The first doodlebug was fired at London on 13 June. Hitler ordered their deployment on the afternoon of D-Day, shortly after hearing of the landings. It took a week to bring the V-1s to launch sites near the Channel. Nearly 10,000 were fired until the last were launched on 29 March 1945. Two thousand, four hundred, and nineteen V-1s did reach London, killing over 6,000 people. Fortunately Allied aircraft, anti-aircraft guns, and barrage balloons combined to bring down 4,261 V-1s. On 8 September, the Germans fired the V-2 on Paris. This weapon was the world's first ballistic missile, with a horizontal range of 200 miles. When fired, it reached a peak altitude of around fifty miles. They were also fired at cities in Belgium, France, and the Netherlands. The last V-2 was launched in March 1945. The weapon is the precursor of modern missile and rocket technology. After the war the Americans recruited Braun. He became one the most important figures in their space programme, helping design the rockets that sent men to the Moon.

7-hour conference

ON 16 JUNE, HITLER FLEW INTO METZ. He then travelled to Margival, north-east of Paris, the site of a *Führer* Headquarters called the *Wolfsschlucht II* ('Wolf's Gorge II'). He had summoned Rommel and Rundstedt for a tactical meeting. The conference began at 09:00 on 17 June. Hitler rounded on the two field marshals, blaming them for allowing the invasion to take place. Rundstedt and Rommel told Hitler that the situation in Normandy was untenable, and there was no chance of driving the Allies back into the sea. They advocated beginning peace talks. Both men demanded to be allowed to pull forces eastward to form a more solid defensive line. They then urged Hitler to use V-1s against the landing beaches or southern English ports. Hitler refused on all fronts. There would be no negotiations. He vowed to use the V-1 to destroy London so that Britain would be forced to sue for peace. Hitler ended the conference at 16:00 by demanding that the army hold fast 'tenaciously to every square yard of soil'.

He had robbed his generals of the flexibility they needed to effectively fight the Allies. Hitler returned to Obersalzberg in Bavaria (the site of his 'Eagle's Nest' headquarters) that evening. On 1 July, Hitler sacked Rundstedt as commander of German forces in the West for his consistent urging to begin peace talks. His replacement was Field Marshal Günther von Kluge. On 17 July, a Spitfire strafed Rommel's car, causing a crash. Rommel was hospitalized with serious injuries and returned to Germany. Kluge took over Rommel's army group, making him the sole commander of German forces in France.

40,549 Allied casualties

DURING THE FIRST TWO WEEKS after the Normandy landings, the Allies suffered 40,549 casualties. The Americans bore the brunt of the damage with 3,082 killed, 13,121 wounded, and 7,959 missing. British forces experienced 1,842 killed, 8,599 wounded, and 3,131 missing, whilst Canadian casualties were 363 killed, 1,359 wounded, and 1,093 missing.

266,804 tons of supplies

ON 22 JUNE, THE AMERICANS began their assault on Cherbourg. As the Americans had been unable to deploy their Mulberry, access to Cherbourg's port would be crucial. As soon as the invasion of France had begun, the Germans had begun to wreck the port. They dumped 20,000 cubic yards of masonry into the harbour basin that could have been used to land large supply ships. After eight days of fighting Cherbourg was captured. It took until August for the Americans to make much use of its port. They landed 266,804 tons and 817 vehicles at Cherbourg, but this was far less than they had hoped. The Americans made heavy use of their landing beaches at Utah and Omaha as ports. Despite having no harbour facilities there, 187,973 tons and 3,986 vehicles were landed at Utah and 351,437 tons and 9,155 vehicles were landed at Omaha.

1,471 sorties

IN 1941, THE ROYAL AIR FORCE established a search and rescue force to save pilots who had ditched over water. Joined by the Americans and other nations, the Allied Air-Sea rescue flew 1,471 sorties in June 1944. In this month they rescued 350 people. On D-Day alone they saved 225 from the waves, including two Germans. Air-sea rescue aircraft accompanied Allied aerial convoys and were able to locate aircrew who had ditched, and either report their location or assist by dropping dinghies. High-speed motor launches were stationed along the route of two 'corridors'. Pilots were briefed on these locations, and knew if they ditched over them, they could be quickly rescued. Thanks to this system very few Allied airmen perished over the Channel.

5 per cent

ONE IN TWENTY VEHICLES taken across the Channel as part of Operation Overlord were lost at sea before they could be brought ashore.

2.5 minutes

THE DENSE BANKS OF HEDGES of the Normandy *bocage* were a major barrier to Allied tank operations. In some places these hedgerows were fifteen feet high. They were thick enough for the Germans to hide machine-gun nests in. The hedges reduced visibility and created bottlenecks at the entries to fields, where the Germans could ambush. Explosives could be used to blast holes through the hedges, but these attracted enemy attention. In early July, Sergeant Curtis G. Culin of the American Second Armoured Division attached sharp 'tusks' made of steel from a German roadblock to the front of his Sherman tank. This enabled it to punch through a hedgerow in just two and a half minutes. Vehicles fitted with the device were nicknamed 'rhino tanks'. The apparatus, made from steel salvaged from German beach defences, was fitted out on the majority of the Second Armoured Division's vehicles in time for Operation Cobra.

670,000,000 cigarettes

THE NAVY, ARMY AND AIR FORCES Institutes (NAAFI) was created in 1921 to cater for the recreational needs of the servicemen of the British Armed Forces. During the war NAAFI was chaired by Lancelot Royle. He had served in the army during World War I and represented Britain as a sprinter in the 1924 Paris Olympics (as part of the famed *Chariots of Fire* relay team). During World War II, Royle oversaw the expansion of NAAFI to a peak of 110,000 personnel. They manned nearly 10,000 establishments. Their clubs, canteens, and shops (as well as the entertainment they organized during the war – employing over 4,000 artists) were essential in boosting the morale of the ranks. NAAFI began operations in France (serving British, Canadian, and American troops) almost as soon as the beachheads were secured. They issued care packages to each soldier, which included cigarettes, matches, soap, shaving kit, cocoa, chewing gum, letter cards, and pencils. By 17 July, they had set up twenty canteens and sent 300 personnel to France. They had landed a total of 670,000,000 cigarettes and 3,300,000 bottles of beer in this period. During the war NAAFI canteens sold an average of 3,500,000 cups of tea and 24,000,000 cigarettes every day.

$135 per pistol

MANY ALLIED SOLDIERS were eager gatherers of German equipment and regalia as battlefield souvenirs, be they found abandoned, collected from the bodies of dead soldiers, or taken from prisoners of war. Much of this souvenir hunting sometimes verged on outright theft or looting. German soldiers were sometimes relieved of personal possessions like jewellery, wristwatches, and even their personal identification books (the *Soldbuch*). As the weather grew colder, overcoats, gloves, and boots were taken to supplement standard-issue uniforms. A valued souvenir was the *Stahlhelm*, the distinctive coal-scuttle-shaped German steel helmet, as were any flags or unit insignia. The most prized item was the Luger pistol, which fetched around $135, nearly three months' basic wage for a private in the US Army. American troops were allowed to have one souvenir pistol in their possession. Anyone carrying more than one faced a court martial and the possibility of being sentenced to six months of hard labour.

117,000 German casualties

BY 16 JULY THE GERMANS had suffered 117,000 casualties in Normandy. They were able to send just 10,000 replacements during this period.

144 pounds

UNLIKE THE GERMANS, who by 1944 were increasingly being forced to rely on young, old, injured, and foreign troops, the Americans were able to be extremely selective when choosing men for military service. So vast was their manpower, the Americans were able to reject one-third of the men called to service for being medically or physically unsuitable in some way. On conscription, the average American soldier weighed 144 pounds and was five feet, eight inches tall. Their average age was twenty-six. After thirteen weeks of basic training they had gained seven pounds in weight (mostly muscle). Half of those drafted into military service had graduated from high school, and ten per cent were university graduates.

8,000 houses left standing

ON 9 JULY, THE ALLIES had finally been able to advance into Caen, capturing the northern part of the city. The British offensive to capture the rest of Caen and break through the German lines to the south was called Operation Goodwood (joined by a simultaneous Canadian assault, Operation Atlantic). The attack started early on 18 July with aerial and artillery bombardments. Next, three armoured divisions rolled towards the German line. Allied losses on the first day were heavy (around 200 tanks were disabled). They were facing some of Germany's best-trained, most fanatical troops, the I SS Panzer Corps. The next day the 500 tanks the Allies held in reserve joined the battle, along with infantry. The Germans held firm and even launched some counter-attacks. On 20 July, Montgomery brought the operation to a halt. The Allies had made gains, including capturing the rest of Caen, but had not made a major breakthrough through the German lines in the area. Caen lay in ruins. Most of its medieval buildings (including the university, established in 1432) had been destroyed. Just 8,000 houses were left standing. By the war's end Caen's population had been reduced from 60,000 to 17,000.

12:42

AS THE WAR DRAGGED ON a group of senior officers in the *Wehrmacht* began to lose faith in Hitler. They planned to assassinate the Führer, freeing the armed forces from their personal oath to him. They would then stage a coup and form a new government that would make peace with the western Allies before the Soviet Union reached Germany. They would use Operation Valkyrie, a German government plan to restore order if there was a state of emergency, to seize positions of power. Killing Hitler was a difficult prospect. He spent most of his time in well-guarded residences and kept his movements secret. No-one with a weapon was allowed near him. One of the conspirators, *Oberst* Claus von Stauffenberg, was a senior official in the Army Reserve, and frequently attended the same meetings as Hitler. Stauffenberg had been severely wounded in North Africa, losing an eye, his right hand and forearm, and two fingers on his left hand. His chance arrived at 12:30 on 20 July. Hitler was holding a staff conference at his *Wolfsschanze* ('Wolf's Lair') headquarters in East Prussia. Stauffenberg had hidden a bomb in his suitcase, which he laid against the leg of a table Hitler was using to view maps. Stauffenberg then left the room, claiming he had to make a call to Berlin. The bomb went off at 12:42. Hitler survived because an officer had moved the suitcase to the other side of the table. He only suffered a cut to the hand and damaged ear drums. With Hitler still alive, the plot fell apart. Stauffenberg and other suspected plotters were captured, tried, and executed. Some were slowly strangled using piano wire. Hitler had these executions filmed so he could watch the recordings. Five thousand people were killed in the purge that followed the assassination attempt.

40 miles gained

BY MID-JULY THE AMERICANS had advanced as far as Saint-Lô. With the Germans tied down at Caen, General Bradley decided the Americans should launch an attack. If the plan, called Operation Cobra, worked then the Americans would be able to advance south into Brittany and be in a position to outflank the Germans. Bradley planned to use fifteen of the twenty-two divisions he had under his command. The operation's beginnings were disastrous. On 24 July, some Allied aircraft carpet-bombing the German lines had accidentally unloaded over American troops, causing 150 casualties. Worse was to come early the next day when Allied bombers caused 600 more friendly-fire casualties. Despite this tragedy, the ground attack began at 11:00. Gains were slow at first. Eventually the Germans began to retreat, falling back fifteen miles by the end of 27 July. To help the Americans maintain their momentum by tying down German forces, the British launched Operation Bluecoat on 30 July. It worked. That day the Americans captured Avranches, which cleared their route into Brittany. On 31 July, Operation Cobra ended. The Allies had advanced forty miles and finally broken out of the confines of the *bocage*. Patton, who would soon re-enter the war effort, had no doubts about the importance of the success of the operation, noting, 'the whole Western Front has been ripped wide open'.

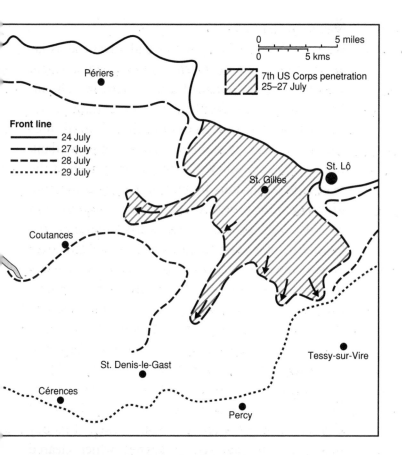

The Plan of Attack for Operation Cobra, 1944

4 field armies

WHEN THE NORMANDY landings began all Allied ground forces in France were part of the Twenty-First Army Group, commanded by Montgomery.

The US First Army, led by Bradley, was initially part of this formation. By 1 August, the Americans had enough men in France to form another field army and a separate American army group. British and Canadian forces would remain part of Montgomery's Twenty-First Army Group. Bradley was promoted to command the newly formed US Twelfth Army Group. General Courtney H. Hodges took over as leader of the US First Army. Commanding the newly activated US Third Army (including the Free French Second Armoured Division, which landed in Normandy on 1 August) would be the famed Patton, who was desperate to play a part in the invasion of France. Eventually two more field armies (the Ninth and Fifteenth) would be added to Bradley's command, making it the largest-ever body of American soldiers (1,300,000 at its peak) gathered under a single leader.

191 German craft lost

THE *KRIEGSMARINE* NAVAL GROUP West oversaw German operations in the waters around France (as well as some coastal artillery units). Its commander-in-chief was Admiral Theodor Krancke. From D-Day to the end of August, Krancke lost 191 ships, a rate of over two every day. Not all were lost in engagements with Allied ships: eighty-eight were lost to air attack and fifty-one were scuttled. On

20 October, the German high command officially dissolved the group.

10,420 American war dogs

ALL OF THE COMBATANT NATIONS used war dogs as sentries, scouts, pack animals, messengers, or mine-seekers (in addition to dogs kept as pets or mascots). The Red Army even trained dogs to run towards armoured targets carrying explosives, which would detonate on impact. When the United States entered the war there was a national campaign encouraging dog owners to volunteer their pets; 10,420 were drafted into service by the Army and Coast Guard. The vast majority were used as sentries. Some dogs were trained to locate buried non-metallic mines, which detectors could not find. The American approach was to run a light electric charge through buried objects that would shock the dogs when they came into contact with them. It was hoped this would teach dogs to fear buried objects and stop when they were located. This was ineffective. In 1944, the Americans discontinued mine-dog training. The British approach was different. They rewarded dogs with food for sniffing out buried unexploded mines, whose scent seeped up through the earth. During training machine guns would be fired and explosives let off to inoculate the dogs to the sound of battle. The British successfully used sixty-four dogs as mine detectors in north-west Europe. The most famed dog who served on the Normandy front worked as a scout – Bing, a two-year-old Alsatian-collie cross. He had been volunteered for military service because rationing restrictions meant his family could no longer feed him. He parachuted into action with the Thirteenth Parachute Battalion of the British Sixth Airborne on D-Day. If he sensed men ahead, he would freeze and point his nose towards the potential danger. Bing acted as a sentry while the men were resting. Despite being wounded by mortar fire, Bing accompanied his battalion through France and into the Ardennes and Germany. After the war he was awarded the Dickin Medal for his gallant service. Bing returned to civilian life and died of natural causes in 1955.

60 victories

DESPITE THE LUFTWAFFE'S superb equipment and numerous experienced pilots, sheer weight of numbers meant they could not match the Allied air forces during the Battle for Normandy. A case in point was Major Hans-Ekkehard Bob, a German fighter pilot. He had claimed sixty victories during the war (this tally is dwarfed by the most successful Luftwaffe pilot, Erich Hartmann, who downed 352 aircraft). During the Battle for Normandy Bob often found himself being pursued by eight to ten Allied fighters at once. This kind of mismatch was by no means uncommon.

150 tanks lost

HITLER CONTINUED TO MEDDLE in military operations. To reverse American gains in Normandy, he ordered a major counter-offensive. Operation Lüttich (the German name for the Belgian city Liège, where they had won a key victory during World War I) would be a surprise attack through Mortain towards Avranches, aimed at splitting the Americans. Kluge told Hitler the plan was doomed, and urged him to allow German forces in Normandy to retreat to the Seine River. Hitler refused. The assault began just after midnight on 7 August. Unbeknownst to the Germans, the Allies had intercepted and decoded the orders to begin Operation Lüttich. The Allies had sent air reinforcements into the area. Once the early morning fog cleared, the Allies quickly won air superiority over the battlefield. Operation Lüttich stalled within a few hours of being launched. The next day the Americans attacked the Germans on their southern flank. At the same time Canadian forces (including the First Polish Armoured Division, which had arrived in Normandy in late July) launched Operation Totalize, attacking the northern flank from Caen. Within a few days the Germans had lost 150 tanks. Their forces in Normandy were now trapped in a pocket around the town of Falaise.

50,000 prisoners taken, 10,000 killed

AFTER THE FAILURE OF Operation Lüttich, around 80,000 Germans were trapped in the Falaise Pocket. The only chance of escape was a narrow gap to the east. Canadian and Polish forces launched Operation Tractable on 14 August to close the gap. The Germans were handed a tactical advantage the night before when a lost Canadian officer carrying the plan of attack was shot driving behind German lines. The captured plans allowed the Germans to reinforce along the Allied line of attack. They fought fiercely to keep the gap open. Hitler, showing his complete ignorance of the reality of the situation, ordered another counter-attack. Kluge, commanding German forces from his headquarters in northern France, refused to do this. On 16 August Kluge was finally allowed to order the men inside the Falaise Pocket to retreat. The next day Hitler sacked Kluge and ordered him back to Berlin, replacing him with Field Marshal Walter Model. Kluge, who had connections with the men in the army who had plotted to kill Hitler, feared arrest and committed suicide by taking cyanide. Rommel was also linked to the plot, and was forced to kill himself on 14 October to protect his family. The German troops in the Falaise Pocket began to retreat under heavy pressure from the Allies. The only road out of the Pocket soon became heavily congested, as a lack of fuel meant numerous vehicles had to be abandoned.

The Allies were able to close the gap on 21 August, cutting off the escape route. Twenty thousand German troops had escaped, along with twenty-five tanks and fifty self-propelled guns. The 50,000 men left in the Pocket were taken prisoner; 10,000 of their compatriots lay dead. The Allied victory at Falaise essentially ended the Battle for Normandy.

30,000 cases of combat exhaustion

FOR MANY ALLIED SOLDIERS the invasion of France was their first experience of combat. They were then flung into battle against a well dug-in, increasingly desperate enemy. Despite their manpower shortages, many of the German soldiers in France had fought in the East. They exported the cunning and brutality of that theatre to Normandy. German snipers were experts at concealing themselves in the countryside. Most of their abandoned positions were laced with lethal booby traps. The dense, high hedgerows, narrow lanes, and small fields that characterized the *bocage* made fighting in Normandy claustrophobic. It is no wonder that many soldiers suffered from combat exhaustion. This made men hypersensitive, irritable, and unable to sleep. The US Army medical services dealt with 30,000 cases of combat exhaustion during the Normandy Campaign.

19,890 civilian casualties

THE PEOPLE OF NORMANDY were caught in the crossfire between the Allies and the desperate German armed forces. Nearly 20,000 civilians were killed during the Battle for Normandy, as well as 15,000 who had died during the Allied bombings of the region prior to D-Day. One hundred and twenty thousand buildings were completely destroyed, and 270,000 had been seriously damaged. Normandy's economy was wrecked – 118,000 acres of farmland were left temporarily unusable and 116,000,000 square feet of factory space was damaged.

Chapter 6:
Aftermath

175,000 Allied soldiers landed in southern France

THE D-DAY LANDINGS were not the only invasion of France to take place in 1944. Operation Dragoon was an Allied invasion of southern France by 175,000 men. It was meant to take place at the same time as the Normandy landings, but it had to be delayed because of slow progress in Italy and a shortage of landing craft. Many Allied leaders, including Churchill, did not support Dragoon. They believed the resources would be better used on offensives in Italy or the Balkans. Eisenhower insisted that Dragoon was essential in pulling away German forces from northern France and providing the Allies with two major ports, Marseille and Toulon. The US Seventh Army led the invasion. Its commander, Major General Alexander Patch, had won victory against the Japanese in the Guadalcanal Campaign (1942–3). Following them would be the Free French

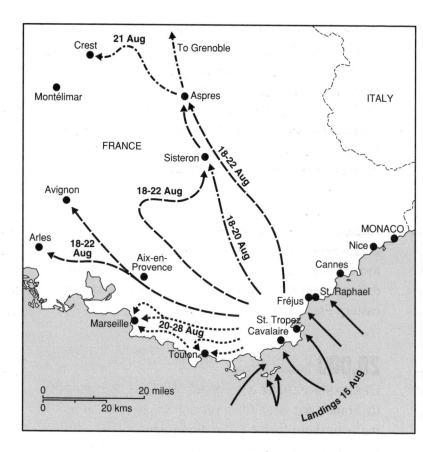

The Invasion Plan for Operation Dragoon, 1944

Army B, led by General Jean de Lattre de Tassigny. The Dragoon landings began on 15 August. They were a resounding success. The Allies, after their experiences at Normandy, had been careful to choose landing beaches with no enemy positions overlooking them. The Allies quickly formed a beachhead. The Germans lacked manpower, and many of their troops were unreliable recruits from the East. Allied paratroopers and Resistance fighters operating behind enemy lines hampered the German fightback. The German commander in southern France, *Generaloberst* Johannes Blaskowitz, had no choice but to retreat. The Free French moved towards Marseille and Toulon, which were liberated on 27 August (both opened to shipping on 20 September). On 3 September, Lyon followed. The Americans moved north, in pursuit of the retreating Germans, driving them all the way to the Vosges Mountains in eastern France by 14 September.

20,000 heads shaved

GERMAN SOLDIERS AND OFFICIALS were stationed in France for over four years. During that time, many of them formed romantic relationships with local women. These liaisons were viewed with hostility by locals. Exacerbating this was the fact that girlfriends and mistresses of Germans often enjoyed better rations and clothing than their neighbours. Whilst the Germans were in control of France these women were protected from public persecution. As the Germans withdrew, many local communities took the chance to shame these women for *collaboration sentimentale*. Sometimes women who had just worked for the Germans or billeted their troops were attacked. The favoured method of doing this was to publicly shave their heads. Sometimes they were beaten, or paraded in the streets, partially stripped with swastikas daubed on their skin. All the while these women were jeered and barracked (such displays of public head-shaving of women who had had relationships with Germans were repeated in Norway, Italy, Belgium, and the Netherlands). In Paris there were reports of prostitutes who had accepted German clients during the occupation being kicked to death. These outbursts of violence again women were part of a wave of violence that took place against all perceived collaborationists, male and female, before the liberation of France. Six thousand people were executed without a formal trial in a wave of violence known as the *épuration sauvage* ('savage purge').

540 miles per hour

THE MESSERSCHMITT ME 262 was the first jet-propelled fighter aircraft. Known as the *Schwalbe* ('Swallow'), it was armed with four cannons and could carry a 500-kilogram bomb load. Delays in development meant it did not enter combat until August 1944. It had a top speed of 540 miles per hour, faster than Allied jet fighters like the British Gloster Meteor.

3,200 Germans killed

AFTER BREAKING OUT OF NORMANDY, the Allied high command did not plan on capturing Paris. The Allies planned on leaving some troops to encircle the city to contain the garrison there and then concentrating on advancing to Germany. This approach would save time and avoid a potentially bloody street-by-street battle in a densely packed urban area. Events in Paris overtook this plan. On 19 August, Paris rose up against the Germans. The German military governor of Paris, *General der Infanterie* Dietrich von Choltitz, had the power of life or death over everyone in the area. Rather than continue the violence Choltitz agreed a truce with the Resistance in Paris. The disorder continued. On 22 August, there were mass strikes and barricades were erected. The Germans had essentially lost control of the city. The capital was ripe for the taking. Under pressure from de Gaulle, Eisenhower allowed General Philippe Leclerc's Free French Second Armoured Division to advance on Paris. On 24 August they entered the Parisian suburbs, with the Americans close behind. Choltitz realized his situation was hopeless. Hitler had ordered him to reduce Paris to ruins before it was captured. He did not follow this command. Choltitz surrendered to the Allies on 25 August. He lost 3,200 men in the fighting, whilst the Allies and the Resistance suffered around 1,000 casualties. Paris had been liberated, and most of its historic buildings and monuments had survived.

$900,000 per annum

MILLIONS OF CONDOMS were distributed to Allied soldiers. Despite the opposition of some religious bodies, they were actively encouraged to use them to avoid sexually transmitted diseases. The official condom supplier to the American armed forces was Julius Schmid, who had emigrated to the United States from Germany in 1882. He had started by making condoms out of animal intestine membranes. Schmid's business took off when he introduced vulcanized rubber condoms to the United States. His 'Fourex', 'Sheik', and 'Ramses' rubber condoms were safe and reliable. Thanks to his contract with the American government, by the end of World War II Schmid's company was earning $900,000 per year. His condoms contributed to the health of the American armed forces (during World War I they had been encouraged to practise restraint, or 'moral prophylaxis', whilst serving overseas, which led to ten per cent of them contracting venereal diseases in France). Condoms were used for more than contraception. Sometimes they were used as water balloons or to waterproof wristwatches and other valuables. Their most practical secondary use was putting them over the muzzle of their rifle barrel to keep out sand and water during the crossing and beach landings on D-Day and other amphibious assaults.

10,000 customers per day

AFTER IT WAS LIBERATED Paris became the favoured destination for Allied soldiers on leave. Many visited the bordellos of the Pigalle (American servicemen nicknamed it 'Pig Alley'), which entertained around 10,000 clients every day.

14,000 pillboxes

IN 1938, HITLER ORDERED the construction of a fortified defensive line protecting Germany's western border. The Siegfried Line (known in German as the *Westwall*) ran 300 miles from the Swiss border to the town of Kleve, near the Dutch frontier. With the Allies closing in on Germany, in August 1944 Hitler drafted in civilian labour (mostly teenage boys) to improve the wall. The line included 14,000 pillboxes, as well as ditches, tank traps, and tunnels.

82 per cent

MANY FRENCH COASTAL TOWNS had been transformed into *Festungen* ('fortresses'). Hitler had ordered their garrisons to stand and fight to the last man. The Allies required these ports to ensure supplies could be shipped to their forces in north-western Europe. On 1 September, Canadian forces had captured Dieppe, the port where their countrymen had suffered such terrible losses during the raid of 1942. On 10 September, Operation Astonia was launched to capture Le Havre. British and Canadian forces liberated it on 12 September, taking 12,000 Germans prisoner. Eighty-two per cent of Le Havre had been destroyed in the fighting. It took a month to make the port operational again. Boulogne fell on 22 September, after a six-day assault. In Brittany, it had taken the Americans over a month to capture Brest, which was liberated on 19 September. The battle for Brest was so long and costly that the Allies decided not to attempt to capture other German-held ports unless it was absolutely necessary. Ports like La Rochelle, Lorient, and Dunkirk would be surrounded so that German forces could not break out, but there would be no attempt to capture them. These cities would not be liberated until the general German surrender in May 1945.

10 square miles of docks,
20 miles of waterfront

THE FAILURE TO CAPTURE several German-held
French ports and the unexpectedly quick advance
through France, led to severe shortages of supplies
for the Allies. The Belgian port of Antwerp offered
a solution. It could handle 1,000 ships and 19,000
tons of cargo per day on its ten square miles of
docks and twenty-mile waterfront. Allied forces
entered Belgium on 2 September. With the help of
the Belgian Resistance, Brussels was captured on 3
September. Antwerp was liberated two days later.
It could not be used right away because German
forces still dominated the northern approaches to
the port.

200 square miles of forest

ON 19 SEPTEMBER, American forces advanced
towards Germany from Belgium. In their way was
the Hürtgen Forest, a 200-square-mile area of man-
made woods, packed with German pillboxes. The
densely planted fir trees and rough terrain meant the
Allies could not effectively use armoured vehicles
or enjoy air support. The Americans were unable
to fight their way through. In mid-December the
Americans suspended operations in the Hürtgen
Forest when the Germans launched the Ardennes
Offensive.

412,193 tons of supplies

WITH THE FRENCH RAILWAYS wrecked, the Allies needed another way to take supplies to the interior of France. On 25 August, the Americans established the Red Ball Express, a truck convoy system between Normandy and their supply base at Chartres. Two routes (one for delivery, one for the route back) were marked out with bollards topped with red balls and closed to civilian traffic. On an average day there were 900 vehicles on the route. Around three-quarters of the drivers were African American. When the Red Ball Express ceased operations on 16 November (when the Allies opened Antwerp to shipping) it had delivered 412,193 tons of supplies.

5,000 *Volkssturm*

AACHEN WAS THE FIRST German city to fall to the Allies. Located close to Germany's border with Belgium and the Netherlands, Aachen was protected by the West Wall. Most of the civilian population had fled the city, which lay in ruins after Allied bombing raids. There were 13,000 German soldiers in the sector. Also entering the fray would be 5,000 members of the *Volkssturm*. Hitler had set up this national militia in October. It was composed of male civilian conscripts aged sixteen to sixty. They received minimal training, mismatched uniforms, and usually had inadequate or outdated weaponry.

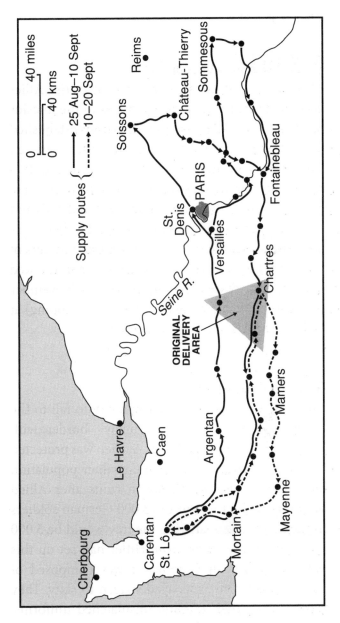

The Route of the Red Ball Express, 1944

Their national commander was Hitler's propaganda chief, Joseph Goebbels, a man with little military experience. On 2 October, American units began an assault on the Aachen area. Despite being grossly outnumbered the Germans fought desperately for every street and house. It took until 21 October for the Americans to force them to surrender.

12,873 casualties to open Antwerp to shipping

AFTER THE NORMANDY CAMPAIGN, the First Canadian Army mostly operated on the French and Belgian coasts. In September they had liberated Dieppe and Boulogne. Calais fell on 1 October. Next was the Scheldt Estuary, on the Dutch-Belgian border. Its banks and three islands on its mouth (Walcheren, North Beveland, and South Beveland) had to be taken to open Antwerp's port. Operation Market-Garden delayed the assault, giving the Germans time to gather weapons and flood the region. Canadian forces marched out of Antwerp on 2 October. The terrain was flat, meaning there was little cover for attacking forces. The damp, water-logged countryside meant the Allies were often unable to use land vehicles. After a series of bloody engagements the Canadians (as well other Allied troops who later served in the campaign – mostly British) made gains along the estuary's banks. North and South Beveland were

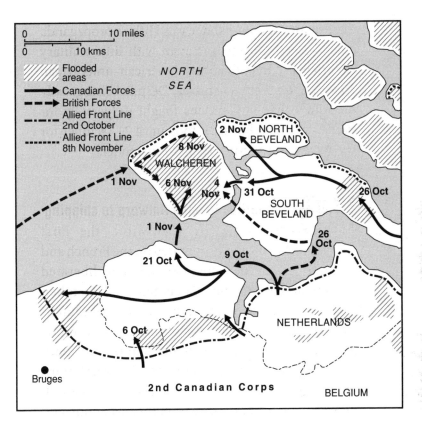

The Battle of the Scheldt, 1944

taken on 2 November. Walcheren remained. The only route to the island was a 7.5 mile causeway around forty yards wide, completely open to the artillery batteries on Walcheren. Despite this, the Canadians secured the causeway, fought their way onto the island, and subdued all German resistance there by 8 November. In total, 41,043 Germans were taken prisoner in the campaign. The final step in clearing the route to Antwerp was sweeping the waters for mines. On 28 November, the first Allied ships entered Antwerp. Leading them was a Canadian-built freighter, the SS *Fort Cataraqui*. Antwerp was vital to the Allies' war effort and solved many of their supply problems. It came at a cost. The Allies suffered 12,873 casualties (half of them Canadian) in securing the Scheldt Estuary.

1,000,000 jerry cans returned

FUEL SUPPLY WAS ONE OF THE MOST crucial aspects of victory. To more quickly distribute petrol, the Allies had developed a machine called the Rotary Cow, which could fill 720 jerry cans per hour. By October 1944, over a million gallons were distributed every day to the Allied armies in France. This relied on the jerry can, which soldiers were supposed to return when emptied. Many neglected to do this, either leaving them behind or using them as stepping stones in the mud. To remedy the shortage, the US Army offered French children prizes and rewards for returning empty jerry cans. This led to the return of over a million jerry cans.

25,602,505 votes won by Roosevelt

ON 7 NOVEMBER, ROOSEVELT won an unprecedented fourth term as president. He polled 3,596,227 more votes than the Republican candidate, Thomas E. Dewey. Roosevelt did not see out his term. He died as the result of a massive stroke on 12 April 1945. The Vice President, Harry S Truman, led the United States for the rest of the war.

10 degrees Celsius

HITLER'S LAST THROW of the dice was Operation Watch on the Rhine, a counter-offensive through the Ardennes Forest. At 05:30 on 16 December, 200,000 German troops advanced on a bulge in the American sector of the line that was undermanned and had many inexperienced troops. They intended to drive all the way to Antwerp, splitting the Allies in two. The attack caught the Americans completely by surprise. To make matters worse, temperatures had dropped to ten degrees below zero, and the American standard-issue uniforms were inadequate to keep out the cold. As the Germans pushed west isolated pockets of soldiers fought valiantly to hold them up. The American bravery was particularly shown at Bastogne, where the Germans completely encircled the 101st American Airborne Division on 20 December. When the German commander demanded their surrender, their acting commander

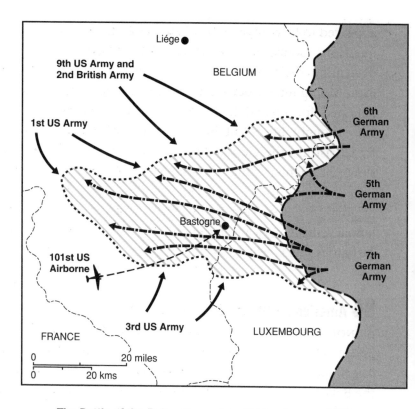

The Battle of the Bulge, December 1944 – January 1945

Brigadier General Anthony McAuliffe simply replied, 'Nuts!' His men held out for a week until they were relieved. To sow suspicion and paranoia, the Germans sent forty-four soldiers dressed in captured US Army uniforms to infiltrate behind enemy lines. It worked. Any unknown people approaching American positions, even if they appeared to be compatriots, often faced numerous questions about life in the United States to determine their true identity. On one occasion even Montgomery, paying a visit to the area, was detained for several hours by American troops who thought he might be an enemy infiltrator. By Christmas the German advance had begun to slow. On 3 January, the Allies launched a counter-attack, forcing the Germans to withdraw to their original line. The Battle of the Bulge ended on 25 January; the Americans had suffered around 80,000 casualties, the Germans around 90,000.

84 American POWs murdered

AT NOON ON 17 DECEMBER, tanks from the First SS Panzer Division intercepted an American convoy of 130 men and thirty vehicles at a crossroads near the Belgian town of Malmédy. The Americans were woefully outgunned. The Germans were part of an elite *Kampfgruppe* ('battle group') commanded by Joachim Peiper, who had already committed numerous atrocities in the East. After a brief firefight, the Americans surrendered. The survivors were assembled in a field and held under guard. For unknown reasons, the SS troops began firing on the prisoners. Men who tried to escape were machine-gunned. Eleven soldiers hid in a nearby cafe. It was set on fire. Those who ran out were shot. After this burst of violence, it is reported that German soldiers roamed the killing field, shooting anyone showing signs of life. Forty-three men managed to escape and return to American lines and reported the massacre. In January 1945, the US Army recovered eighty-four corpses from the site. Autopsies confirmed the survivors' accounts. As news of the murders spread, many Americans resolved to kill any German prisoners. On New Years' Day 1945, American soldiers massacred around thirty German prisoners at Chenogne, Belgium, in retaliation for Malmédy.

5,000 volunteers

THE ARDENNES COUNTER-OFFENSIVE stretched the Americans. In December 1944, Lieutenant General John C. H. Lee, in charge of logistics for the US Army in Europe, took a radical step. He allowed all black soldiers with basic training to volunteer for frontline infantry units. He planned to have them serve alongside white soldiers. Eisenhower, mindful that segregation in the army was a federal law, insisted that they serve in all-black platoons. Five thousand black soldiers volunteered. Almost without exception they were effective front-line troops, making a mockery of the US Army's policy of excluding black soldiers from combat. To this point the only trained African-American combat unit in the US Army was the 761st Tank Battalion (nicknamed the Black Panthers). They landed in France in October 1944. The 761st served with distinction and were involved in the fightback at the Battle of the Bulge.

30,000 prisoners of war per month

BETWEEN D-DAY AND Christmas 1944, an average of 30,000 German prisoners of war were sent to American camps every month. In Texas thirty-three facilities were built to house them. The average size of a German prisoner was five feet, five-and-three-quarter inches, with a weight of around 150 pounds. Their average age was twenty-eight.

20,000,000 food parcels

THE AXIS POWERS IN EUROPE allowed Allied prisoners of war to receive Red Cross food parcels to supplement their monotonous and increasingly meagre rations. The Japanese did not allow Red Cross ships to travel through their waters, so prisoners in their hands, held in harsh and brutal conditions, did not receive any food packages. During the war the British Red Cross and the Order of Saint John of Jerusalem sent out 20,000,000 parcels to Allied prisoners of war. They included a quarter of a pound of tea, a tin of dried eggs, tobacco, and a bar of soap. The packages were shipped to Lisbon or Marseille, then sent on to Geneva for distribution by the International Red Cross. The American and Canadian Red Cross also sent packages (27,000,000 and 16,500,000, respectively).

488 divisions

AT THE BEGINNING OF 1945, the Soviet Union had 488 divisions available. Although Germany had 319 divisions to call on, most of them were understrength and undermanned. The Germans faced a multi-front war, and could only commit half of their divisions to fighting off the Soviets. The Red Army had one clear goal: to destroy the Third Reich. On 31 January, the Soviets crossed the German frontier with Berlin firmly in their sights.

3 overflowing platefuls of cake

HITLER MOVED PERMANENTLY to the *Führerbunker*, near the Reich Chancellery in Berlin, on 16 January 1945. Thirteen feet of concrete protected the bunker whilst diesel generators kept it supplied with light and ventilation. Hitler's health deteriorated rapidly. His mental state vacillated from gloomy fatalism to a deluded optimism that the Western–Soviet

Alliance would break down or a 'miracle weapon' would win the war. Usually prim and neat, Hitler's clothing became bedraggled and dirty. It was often covered in crumbs, as during the final months of the war Hitler had become, in the words of a fellow bunker resident, a 'cake-devouring wreck'. One of his secretaries reported that his desire for cake had become pathological. Always a man with a sweet tooth, Hitler had usually stopped at three pieces of cake in a sitting but by 1945 had to fill his plate to overflowing three times to be satisfied. Even though defeat was increasingly certain Hitler refused to surrender. On 19 March, he issued the Nero Decree, ordering the destruction of Germany's infrastructure. Albert Speer, Hitler's favourite architect and Minister for Armaments, was to carry out the order. Speer refused to and, without Hitler's knowledge, used his influence to prevent the decree being followed.

5 elections never held

FROM 4–11 FEBRUARY, Stalin, Roosevelt, and Churchill met at the Crimean resort city of Yalta, on the Black Sea. It was decided that after the war Germany would be divided into American, British, French, and Soviet occupation zones. There would also be an international court to try Nazi war criminals. Stalin agreed that the Soviet Union would declare war against Japan two or three months after Germany surrendered. All sides agreed to hold free democratic elections in liberated and former Axis satellite nations. Stalin failed to live up to this promise. Elections were never held in Poland, Czechoslovakia, Hungary, Romania, and Bulgaria, where unelected Communist regimes friendly to the Soviet Union were installed.

18 days

THE LUDENDORFF RAILWAY BRIDGE at Remagen was one of the few crossings of the River Rhine that the Germans had not destroyed. Under heavy fire, the American Ninth Armoured Division captured the bridge on 7 March. Rather than use pontoons or boats, the Allies poured across the Ludendorff Bridge. They established a bridgehead on the east bank of the Rhine and poured into the industrial Ruhr region. So heavy was the traffic that the bridge collapsed on 17 March. The Americans moved in a pincer movement around German Army Group B. The 430,000 men were fully encircled on 4 April in an area called the Ruhr Pocket. Hitler ordered them to fight to the last man, and neither surrender nor attempt to break out. Fighting in the Pocket would continue for eighteen days. The German commander was Field Marshal Walter Model, nicknamed the 'Führer's

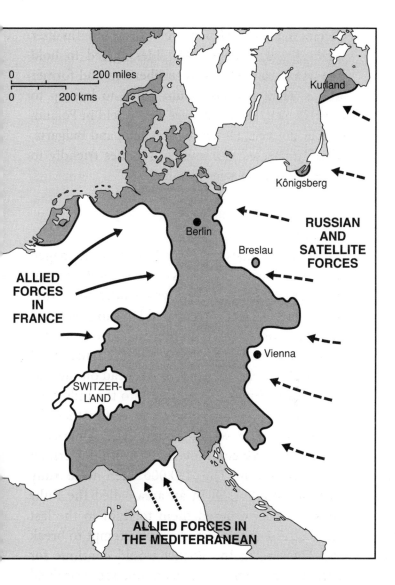

The Western Allied and Soviet Advance into Germany, 1945

Fireman' for his ability to rescue dire situations. There was nothing he could do to save this one. Even though defeat was certain, Model, mindful of his oath to obey Hitler's orders, refused to formally surrender. Instead he discharged old and young soldiers. Everyone else was permitted to surrender or try and break out, if they wished. On 21 April, Model committed suicide by shooting himself in the head. The fighting in the Pocket ended that day; the surviving 325,000 German soldiers were taken prisoner.

4 Tiger I Tanks

THE COASTAL CITY OF DANZIG (also known as Gdańsk) was a major shipping and industrial centre. Albert Forster, the local Nazi Party leader (*Gauleiter*), was responsible for the deportation and death of thousands of Jews and non-Germans in the region. In mid-March the Red Army was poised to attack Danzig. Forster rushed to Berlin for help. In an audience with Hitler he claimed to only have four Tiger I tanks to defend the city. The Soviets had 1,100 tanks poised to strike. Hitler convinced Forster that Danzig would be saved. His assurances were baseless. Danzig fell on 28 March. After the war Forster was tried for war crimes and executed by hanging in 1952.

12-year-old recipient of the Iron Cross

THE FÜHRER's FINAL public appearance was on 20 April, his fifty-sixth birthday. After a desultory reception Hitler awarded the Iron Cross medal for bravery to nineteen boys in a ceremony outside of his bunker. Germany awarded the Iron Cross for bravery or leadership in the face of the enemy (Hitler had been awarded one himself during World War I). The youngest of the boys to be honoured was Alfred Czech, a twelve-year-old member of the *Jungvolk* from rural Silesia. He had saved a group of German soldiers under Soviet attack by rescuing them on his father's cart. Czech was flown to Berlin for the ceremony. Hitler pinched his cheek and asked him if he was afraid when he saved the soldiers. Czech answered, 'No, my Führer!' Hitler told the boys, 'Despite the gravity of these times, I remain firmly convinced that we will achieve victory in this battle.' After the ceremony the boys dined with Hitler before being sent to the battlefront with their Iron Crosses pinned to their tunics. In the fighting Czech was shot in the lung. He was later detained in a prisoner of war camp in Czechoslovakia. After being freed he walked home in 1947 to find his village was in Poland. Czech emigrated to West Germany in 1964 and lived quietly as a building labourer. He was one of nearly five million people awarded an Iron Cross during World War II. By the closing days of the war heavy crates of the medals were being used to barricade windows in the Reich Chancellery.

14,000 pounds of human hair

THE SOVIETS WERE THE FIRST of the Allies to discover a Nazi extermination camp: Maidanek in Poland, near the city of Lublin. Before evacuating it, the Nazis had tried to hide their activities there by setting fire to parts of the camp but they had left the gas chambers standing. The Red Army then found Belzec, Sobibor, and Treblinka. These camps had been dismantled the year before. The largest extermination camp, Auschwitz-Birkenau, where over one million people had been killed, was liberated in January 1945. The Nazis had begun moving prisoners into the interior of Germany in brutal death marches, so the Soviets found only a few thousand prisoners alive in Auschwitz-Birkenau. At the camp the Soviets found warehouses full of the personal belongings of the prisoners, including 800,000 women's outfits and over 14,000 pounds of human hair (used to make felt, thread, ropes, cords, socks for U-boat crews, and stuffing for mattresses). As the Red Army advanced west, they found more camps in Poland and the Baltic. If they did find any survivors, they were mostly skeletal and barely able to move. The western Allies also found the evidence of the Nazi's heinous crimes as they advanced into the interior of Germany. The US Army found the largest concentration camp complex in Germany, Buchenwald, near Weimar, on 11 April 1945. The prisoners at Buchenwald had risen up to prevent the remaining camp guards killing them before the Allies arrived. Over 20,000 prisoners were freed there. Four days later the British liberated Bergen-Belsen in northern Germany. They found 60,000 prisoners in the midst of a typhus epidemic. In the subsequent weeks, over 10,000 died from disease or malnutrition. During the Holocaust the Nazis had murdered over six million Jews from across Europe. They also killed five million non-Jews who were seen as enemies of the Third Reich, including Roma, Jehovah's Witnesses, political opponents, resistance fighters, freemasons, homosexuals, and disabled people.

118,216 square miles gained

THE US THIRD ARMY was perhaps the most successful Allied formation in the European campaign. From August 1944 to May 1945, Patton had led a total of 500,000 men, and gained 118,216 square miles of land in France, Luxembourg, Belgium, Germany, Czechoslovakia, and Austria. They took 1,280,688 prisoners and caused 1,443,888 casualties.

372,000 surrendered in Scandinavia

THE BRITISH DECEPTION CAMPAIGN had made Hitler so convinced that there might be an invasion through Scandinavia that he had kept thousands of men there even as the Allies swept through France and into Germany. At the end of the war 372,000 German troops were still stationed there.

39 cubic yards of rubble per person

ON 16 APRIL, THE RED ARMY had broken through to the suburbs of Berlin. Three days before they had conquered Vienna but Berlin was the prize Stalin was desperate to win. During the battle for the city the desperate German high command flung almost anyone into the fray. Thirty thousand German teenagers died in the attempt to save Berlin. The city was in ruins. For every person living there, there were around thirty-nine cubic yards of rubble. In the previous two years the Western Allies had dropped 65,000 tons of explosive bombs on the city. During just the last two weeks of April the closing Russian armies had unleashed 40,000 tons of ordnance on the shattered capital of the Third Reich. With defeat certain, Hitler committed suicide in his bunker on 30 April. Goebbels followed his example the next day. On 2 May, German forces in Berlin surrendered to the Allies. Before he died, Hitler made Grand Admiral Karl Dönitz, commander of the *Kriegsmarine*, his successor as President of Germany. His short-lived provisional government was based in Flensburg, a town in northern Germany. On 7 May, Dönitz gave Jodl permission to sign an unconditional surrender that brought the war in Europe to an end. All German forces were ordered to stop operations on 8 May, which was celebrated as Victory in Europe Day.

939,061 explosive devices cleared

THE BRITISH CORPS of Royal Engineers disposed of 939,061 unexploded bombs and mines in the eleven months between the Normandy landings and the end of the war – a daily average of nearly three thousand.

5 Ds

ON 17 JULY, THE ALLIED LEADERS met at Potsdam, outside of Berlin. Of the original 'Big Three' only Stalin would finish the conference. Truman was now President and midway through the meetings Clement Attlee replaced Churchill as Prime Minister after his victory in the 1945 British General Election. On 26 July, the conference issued the Potsdam Declaration, an ultimatum demanding Japan's unconditional surrender on threat of 'prompt and utter destruction'. An Allied Control Council was set up to administer matters concerned with the occupation of Austria and Germany. The council's five core policies were known as the 'Five Ds': demilitarization, denazification, democratization, decentralization, and deindustrialization. The conference ended on 2 August. There had been a distinct lack of cooperative spirit. Stalin was becoming increasingly unwilling to make concessions or allow any interference in eastern Europe. After Potsdam tensions increased between the Soviets and the West, meaning it would be the last meeting of all the Allies.

34.5 kilotons of nuclear weapons

THE MANHATTAN PROJECT was the US Army Corps of Engineers' top-secret project to develop nuclear weapons (with British and Canadian assistance). The first successful test of an atomic device was carried out on 16 July 1945 at Alamogordo, New Mexico. After the Japanese government ignored the Potsdam Declaration, atomic weapons were used to bring the war in the Pacific to a close. Truman wanted to avoid a potentially bloody invasion of Japan, which he had been advised would lead to one million American casualties. The first target was the city of Hiroshima. On 6 August, a modified

B-29 called the *Enola Gay* parachuted a nuclear bomb (code-named 'Little Boy) over the city. It exploded with the force of 12,500 tons of TNT. The Japanese government refused to surrender. On 9 August, another B-29, *Bockscar*, set out over Japan with a larger device, the 'Fat Man', which had the power of 22,000 tons of TNT. There was thick cloud over the primary target, Kokura, so the bomb was dropped over the city of Nagasaki. Over 150,000 people were killed in the blasts. Six days after the attack on Nagasaki, Emperor Hirohito of Japan announced his country's surrender. On 2 September, the Japanese Instrument of Surrender was signed on the deck of the aircraft carrier USS *Missouri*, anchored in Tokyo Bay. This act formally ended the war.

$185,000,000,000 in war bonds

THE UNITED STATES essentially bankrolled and supplied much of the Allied war effort, spending $300,000,000,000 fighting the Axis. Many in the government wanted to raise money through payroll taxes. However, the Secretary of the Treasury, Henry Morgenthau, Jr., wanted to finance the war using voluntary loans from the American people. The Treasury Department began issuing War Bonds. Under this programme, people could purchase bonds at seventy-five per cent of face value. The money from the bond would then go to financing the war effort. Ten years after purchase the government would redeem the bond for its full value, although they could accrue interest for up to forty years. There was a national poster campaign, travelling shows, and radio broadcasts all exhorting the American people to purchase war bonds. Even children could play a role by buying 'War Stamps' for twenty-five cents to paste into booklets. By the end of the war, the American people had purchased $185,000,000,000 in bonds. Total bond purchases in Canada during the war were over C$2,000,000,000. In 1942, an event called 'If Day' was staged to promote the sale of war bonds. A German invasion of the city of Winnipeg was staged to show the impact of Nazi victory on daily life. Volunteers and actors dressed as German soldiers paraded through the streets, books were burned, the swastika was raised over the city, and prominent local politicians were interned.

92 countries involved

DURING THE SIX YEARS of World War II ninety-two nations were involved in the fighting. The last country to formally enter the conflict was the Mongolian People's Republic, which joined the Allies on 9 August 1945.

13 Nuremberg Trials

ON 8 AUGUST, the Allies issued the London Charter setting out the procedures for the prosecution of war criminals. The trials were to be held in the Bavarian city of Nuremberg, scene of the largest Nazi rallies. First to be tried were twenty-three of the most important wartime German leaders, known as the 'Major War Criminals'. They included Hermann Göring, the commander of the Luftwaffe; Dönitz; and two of the most important *Wehrmacht* leaders, Jodl and Wilhelm Keitel. Joachim von Ribbentrop, the foreign minister, and Speer were also tried. Martin Bormann, Hitler's private secretary, was tried *in absentia* (in 1972 his remains were found in Berlin, where he had died during the closing days of the war). One of those indicted, Robert Ley, head of the German Labour Front, hung himself using an improvised noose made of strips of towel before proceedings began. The trial began on 20 November 1945. The defendants all entered not-guilty pleas. The verdicts were delivered on 1 October 1946. Three were acquitted, seven were sentenced to prison terms, and twelve were sentenced to death by hanging (including Jodl, Keitel, Ribbentrop, and Bormann *in absentia*). On 15 October, Göring committed suicide before he could be executed. He swallowed a cyanide pill that was smuggled in to him hidden in a jar of skin medication.

The next day the executions of the remaining ten were carried out. There were twelve more trials. Each was concerned with a specific group, including doctors who had carried out human experimentation and mass murder, legal figures who had supported the Nazi regime, industrialists who were accused of using slave labour, and high-ranking military officials. These trials went on until 1949, indicting 185 people. Twelve of them were sentenced to death and another eighty-five received prison sentences.

9,387 buried

AFTER THE WAR ENDED one of the first considerations was to establish permanent resting places for the soldiers who had died. There was no time to send corpses home, so most had been buried in temporary cemeteries established near to battlefields. In the years after the war there was a transnational effort to exhume bodies from temporary burial sites scattered across Normandy to permanent cemeteries. The largest resting place for Allied troops who died during D-Day and its subsequent operations is the Normandy American Cemetery and Memorial in France. It overlooks Omaha Beach, and is near to the site of a temporary cemetery established on 8 June 1944. Today the cemetery covers 172.5 acres and contains the graves of 9,387 military dead. The names of 1,557 soldiers whose bodies could not be located are inscribed on a wall in a garden in the cemetery. The largest Commonwealth cemetery is just outside Bayeux. The cemetery there was completed in 1952; it contains 4,144 Commonwealth graves, as well as 505 from other countries. Opposite the cemetery is the Bayeux Memorial, which is engraved with the names of the 1,808 Commonwealth soldiers who died during the Normandy Campaign whose bodies could not be found. The largest German cemetery in Normandy is located nearby, at La Cambe; 21,222 are buried there.

65 million dead

WHEN THE FIGHTING finally finished, World War II cost over sixty-five million lives, making it by far the costliest conflict in history. The actual figure may be higher, as civilian deaths cannot be exactly calculated, but they are thought to have numbered between thirty and fifty-five million. In total this was at least two per cent of the world's population. Around 20,280,000 of the casualties were military personnel. Twelve million of them were from the Soviet Union. Over the course of the war, a total of nearly one hundred and twenty-one million people fought in the armed forces. Around forty per cent of them (47,980,000) were wounded. Over five million vehicles and nearly 800,000 aircraft were produced during the conflict. The war caused unprecedented damage from the Arctic Circle to the Sahara Desert. In addition to the lives lost, World War II left hundreds of millions more people injured, homeless, or bereaved across the globe. Despite knowing the huge costs of total, fully mechanized war, humanity remained unable to renounce violence. From the conflict's ashes emerged an era of suspicion and paranoia, as the Soviet- and American-dominated power blocs vied with each other for world domination.

SELECT BIBLIOGRAPHY

Absolute Victory: America's Greatest Generation and Their World War II Triumph (Time-Life Books)

Ambrose, Stephen E., *D-Day June 6, 1944: The Climactic Battle of World War II* (Simon & Schuster)

Axelrod, Alan, *Encyclopedia of World War II* (Facts on File)

Badsey, Stephen, *Normandy 1944: Allied Landings and Breakout* (Osprey)

Balkoski, Joseph, *Omaha Beach: D-Day, June 6, 1944* (Stackpole Books)

Beevor, Anthony, *D-Day: The Battle for Normandy* (Viking)

Bickers, Richard, *Air War Normandy* (Pen and Sword Books)

Cawthorne, Nigel, *Fighting Them on the Beaches: The D-Day Landings June 6, 1944* (Arcturus)

Chandler, D.G., and Collins, Jr. J.L., eds., *The D-Day Encyclopedia* (Simon & Schuster)

Fey, William, *Armour Battles of the Waffen-SS* (Stackpole Books)

Ford, Ken, *D-Day 1944 (3) Sword Beach and British Airborne Landings* (Osprey)

Ford, Ken, *D-Day 1944 (4) Gold and Juno Beaches* (Osprey)

Granatstein, J.L., *Canada's Army: Waging War and Keeping the Peace* (University of Toronto Press)

Holmes, Richard, *The D-Day Experience: From the Invasion to the Liberation of Paris* (Carlton Books)

Koskimaki, George, *D-Day with the Screaming Eagles* (Presidio Press)

Lewis, Adrian R., *Omaha Beach: A Flawed Victory* (University of North Carolina Press)

Martin, C., *World War II Book of Lists* (The History Press)

McManus, John C., *The Americans at D-Day: The American Experience at the Normandy Invasion* (Forge Books)

Messenger, Charles, *The D-Day Atlas: Anatomy of the Normandy Campaign* (Thames & Hudson)

Neillands, Robin, *The Battle of Normandy, 1944* (Cassell)

Paterson, Lawrence, *Black Flag: The Surrender of Germany's U-Boat Forces* (MBI Publishing Company)

Rogers, J., and Rogers, D., *D-Day Beach Force: The Men Who Turned Chaos Into Order* (The History Press)

Ryan, Cornelius, *The Longest Day: The Classic Epic of D-Day* (Simon & Schuster)

Willmott, H.P., *et al, World War II* (Dorling Kindersley)

Zaloga, Steven J., *Rangers Lead the Way: Pointe-du-Hoc D-Day 1944* (Osprey)

Zuehlke, Mark, *Juno Beach: Canada's D-Day Victory: June 6, 1944* (Douglas & McIntyre)

INDEX

Locations of illustrations are shown in italics.

Named operations are listed under 'Operations.'

Regiments etc. whose number is represented in figures are indexed numerically at the head of this index. Other regiments are indexed alphabetically within the index. All regiments are British unless otherwise denoted.